GUAN YU

BLOOD BROTHERS TO THE END

A CHINESE LEGEND

GRAPHIC UNIVERSE™

STORY BY
DAN JOLLEY
PENCILS AND INKS BY
RON RANDALL

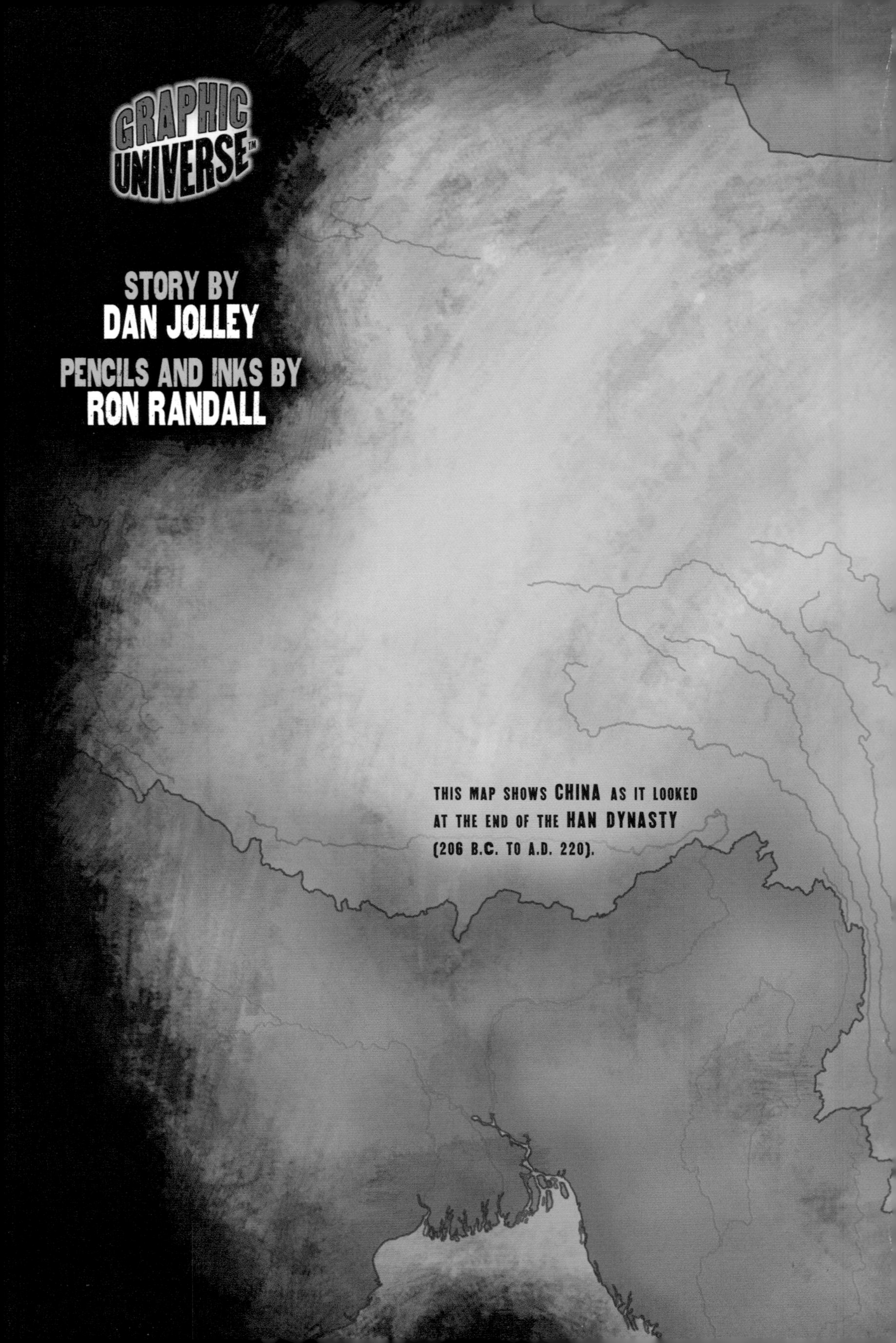

THIS MAP SHOWS CHINA AS IT LOOKED AT THE END OF THE HAN DYNASTY (206 B.C. TO A.D. 220).

GUAN YU

BLOOD BROTHERS TO THE END

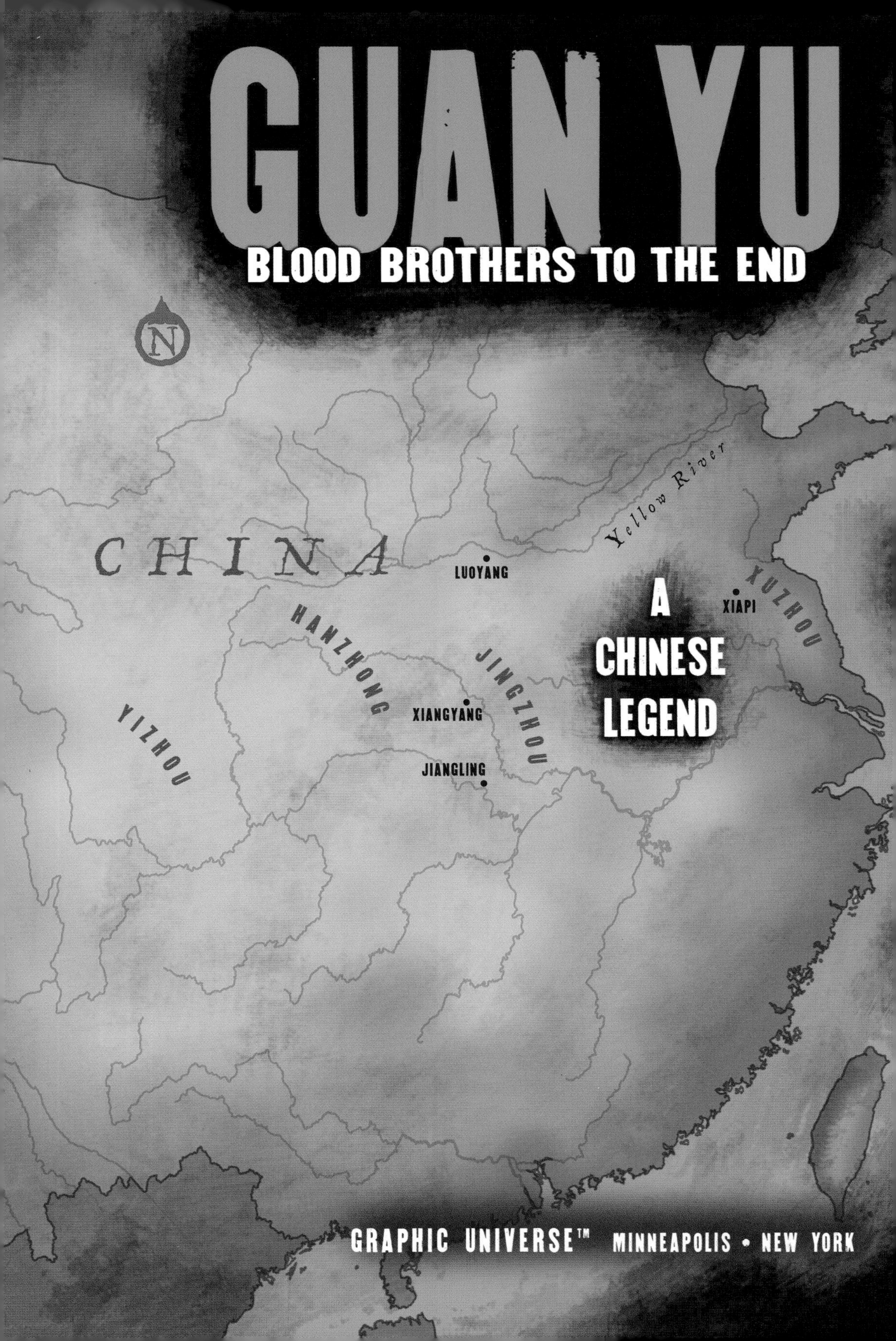
N
CHINA
Yellow River
LUOYANG
XIAPI
XUZHOU
HANZHONG
JINGZHOU
XIANGYANG
YIZHOU
JIANGLING

A CHINESE LEGEND

GRAPHIC UNIVERSE™ MINNEAPOLIS • NEW YORK

GUAN YU WAS AN ANCIENT CHINESE WARRIOR. HE IS ALSO AN IMPORTANT FIGURE IN *THE ROMANCE OF THE THREE KINGDOMS*, A FOURTEENTH-CENTURY NOVEL ATTRIBUTED TO CHINESE WRITER LUO GUANZHONG. LUO'S NOVEL DESCRIBES THE ACTIVITIES OF WARRIORS IN THE YEARS FOLLOWING THE HAN DYNASTY (206 B.C. TO A.D. 220).

THIS ADAPTATION OF GUAN YU'S STORY IS BASED PRIMARILY ON *THREE KINGDOMS: A HISTORICAL NOVEL*, TRANSLATED BY MOSS ROBERTS. IT WAS WRITTEN IN CONSULTATION WITH WANG PING, PHD, ASSOCIATE PROFESSOR OF ENGLISH AT MACALESTER COLLEGE, AND WEN-HUA DU, MA, OF THE DEPARTMENT OF FOREIGN LANGUAGES AND LINGUISTICS AT THE UNIVERSITY OF WISCONSIN-MILWAUKEE. THE ARTWORK FOR THE BOOK IS BASED ON NUMEROUS HISTORICAL RESOURCES AND WAS REVIEWED FOR ACCURACY BY WANG PING.

STORY BY DAN JOLLEY

PENCILS AND INKS BY RON RANDALL

COLORING BY HI-FI COLOUR DESIGN

LETTERING BY MARSHALL DILLON
AND TERRI DELGADO

CONSULTANTS: WANG PING, PHD,
ASSOCIATE PROFESSOR OF ENGLISH,
MACALESTER COLLEGE,
AND WEN-HUA DU, MA,
DEPARTMENT OF FOREIGN LANGUAGES AND
LINGUISTICS, UNIVERSITY OF WISCONSIN—MILWAUKEE

Copyright © 2008 by Lerner Publishing Group, Inc.

Graphic Universe™ is a trademark of Lerner Publishing Group, Inc.

Graphic Universe™
A division of Lerner Publishing Group, Inc.
241 First Avenue North
Minneapolis, MN 55401 USA

For reading levels and more information look up this title at www.lernerbooks.com.

Library of Congress Cataloging-in-Publication Data

Jolley, Dan.
    Guan Yu : blood brothers to the end : a Chinese legend / story by Dan Jolley ; pencils and inks by Ron Randall.
      p.   cm. — (Graphic myths and legends)
    Includes index.
    ISBN 978-0-8225-7527-6 (lib. bdg. : alk. paper)
    ISBN 978-0-7613-3994-6 (EB pdf)
    1. Luo, Guanzhong, ca. 1330–ca. 1400. San guo zhi yan yi. 2. Guan, Yu, 160–220—Fiction. 3. China—History—Three kingdoms, 220–265—Fiction. I. Randall, Ron. II. Title.
PL2690.S33J65 2008
741.5'973—dc22   2007019742

Manufactured in the United States of America
5-48073-8453-7/3/2019

TABLE OF CONTENTS

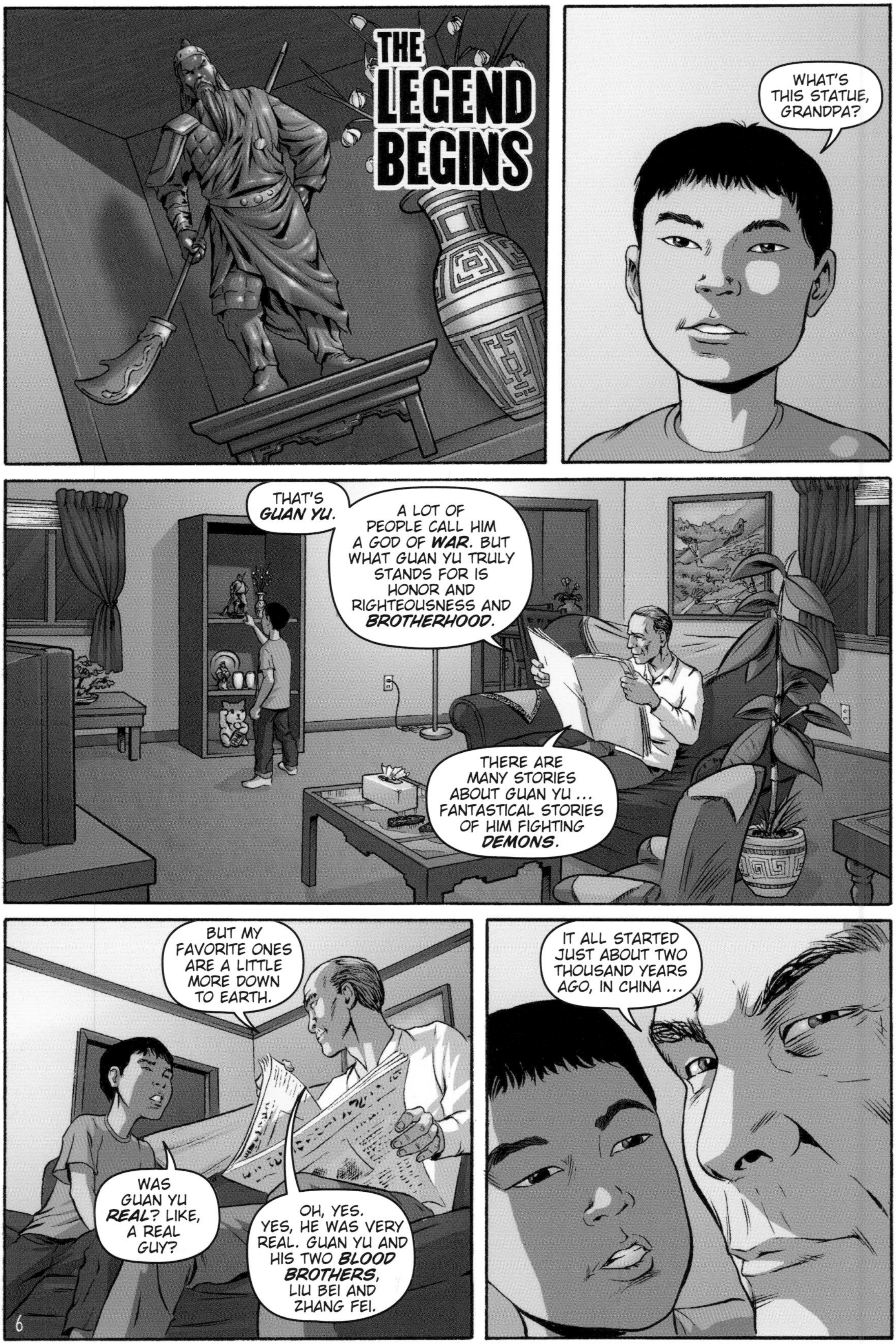
THE LEGEND BEGINS
WHAT'S THIS STATUE, GRANDPA?
THAT'S *GUAN YU*.
A LOT OF PEOPLE CALL HIM A GOD OF *WAR*. BUT WHAT GUAN YU TRULY STANDS FOR IS HONOR AND RIGHTEOUSNESS AND *BROTHERHOOD*.
THERE ARE MANY STORIES ABOUT GUAN YU ... FANTASTICAL STORIES OF HIM FIGHTING *DEMONS*.
BUT MY FAVORITE ONES ARE A LITTLE MORE DOWN TO EARTH.
WAS GUAN YU *REAL*? LIKE, A REAL GUY?
OH, YES. YES, HE WAS VERY REAL. GUAN YU AND HIS TWO *BLOOD BROTHERS*, LIU BEI AND ZHANG FEI.
IT ALL STARTED JUST ABOUT TWO THOUSAND YEARS AGO, IN CHINA ...

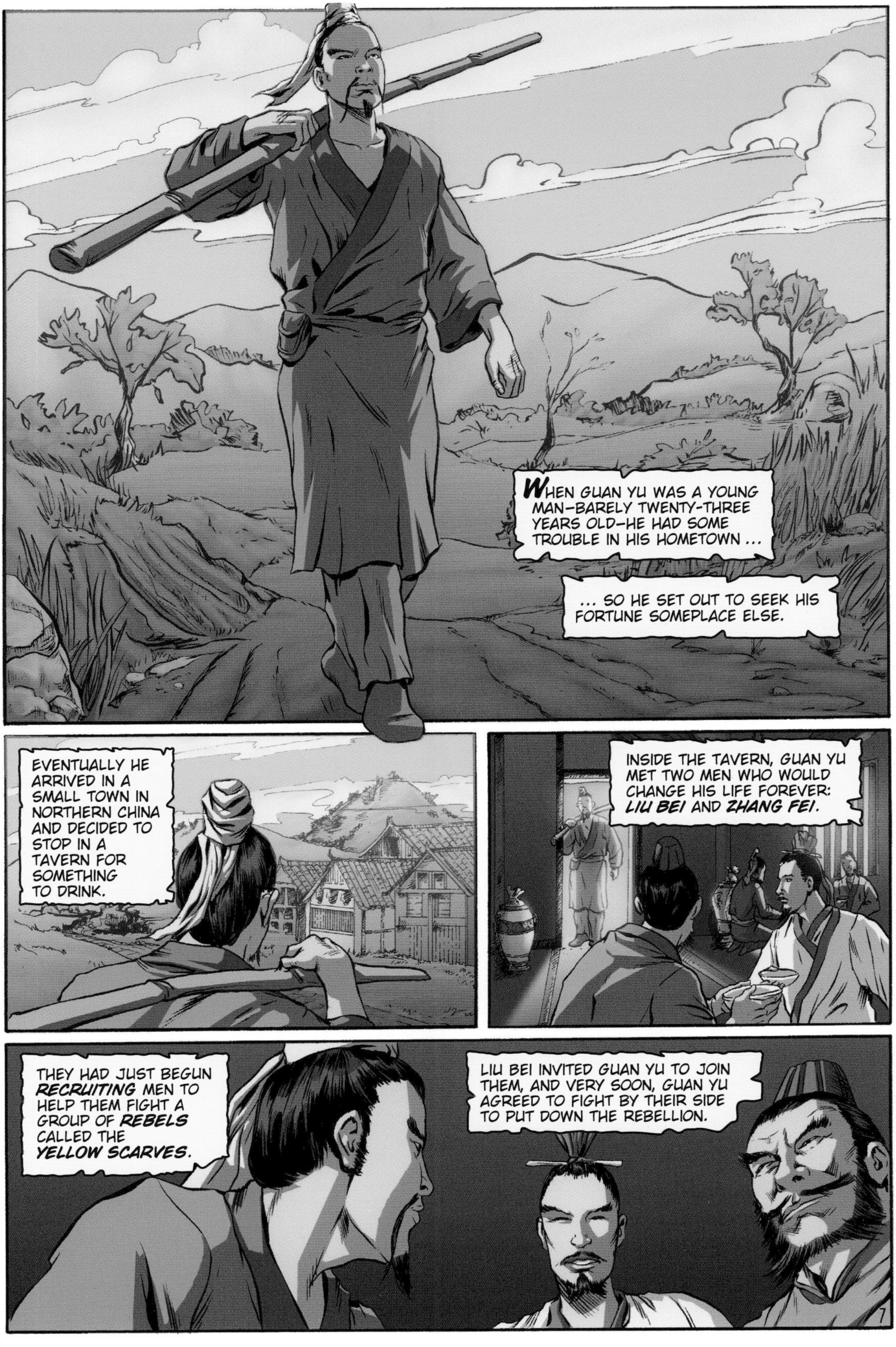
WHEN GUAN YU WAS A YOUNG MAN—BARELY TWENTY-THREE YEARS OLD—HE HAD SOME TROUBLE IN HIS HOMETOWN ...
... SO HE SET OUT TO SEEK HIS FORTUNE SOMEPLACE ELSE.
EVENTUALLY HE ARRIVED IN A SMALL TOWN IN NORTHERN CHINA AND DECIDED TO STOP IN A TAVERN FOR SOMETHING TO DRINK.
INSIDE THE TAVERN, GUAN YU MET TWO MEN WHO WOULD CHANGE HIS LIFE FOREVER: LIU BEI AND ZHANG FEI.
THEY HAD JUST BEGUN RECRUITING MEN TO HELP THEM FIGHT A GROUP OF REBELS CALLED THE YELLOW SCARVES.
LIU BEI INVITED GUAN YU TO JOIN THEM, AND VERY SOON, GUAN YU AGREED TO FIGHT BY THEIR SIDE TO PUT DOWN THE REBELLION.

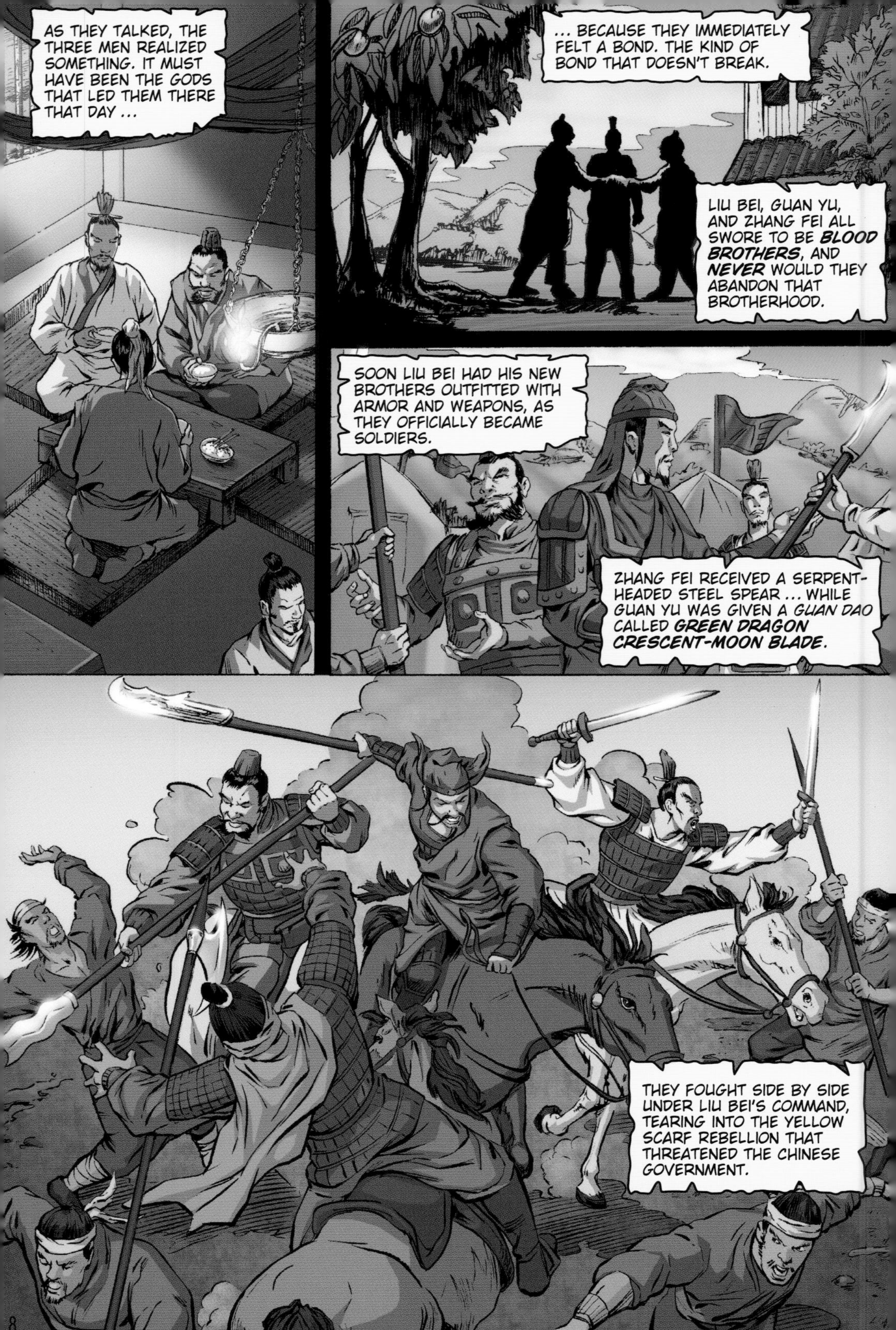
AS THEY TALKED, THE THREE MEN REALIZED SOMETHING. IT MUST HAVE BEEN THE GODS THAT LED THEM THERE THAT DAY . . .
. . . BECAUSE THEY IMMEDIATELY FELT A BOND. THE KIND OF BOND THAT DOESN'T BREAK.
LIU BEI, GUAN YU, AND ZHANG FEI ALL SWORE TO BE **BLOOD BROTHERS**, AND **NEVER** WOULD THEY ABANDON THAT BROTHERHOOD.
SOON LIU BEI HAD HIS NEW BROTHERS OUTFITTED WITH ARMOR AND WEAPONS, AS THEY OFFICIALLY BECAME SOLDIERS.
ZHANG FEI RECEIVED A SERPENT-HEADED STEEL SPEAR . . . WHILE GUAN YU WAS GIVEN A *GUAN DAO* CALLED ***GREEN DRAGON CRESCENT-MOON BLADE***.
THEY FOUGHT SIDE BY SIDE UNDER LIU BEI'S COMMAND, TEARING INTO THE YELLOW SCARF REBELLION THAT THREATENED THE CHINESE GOVERNMENT.

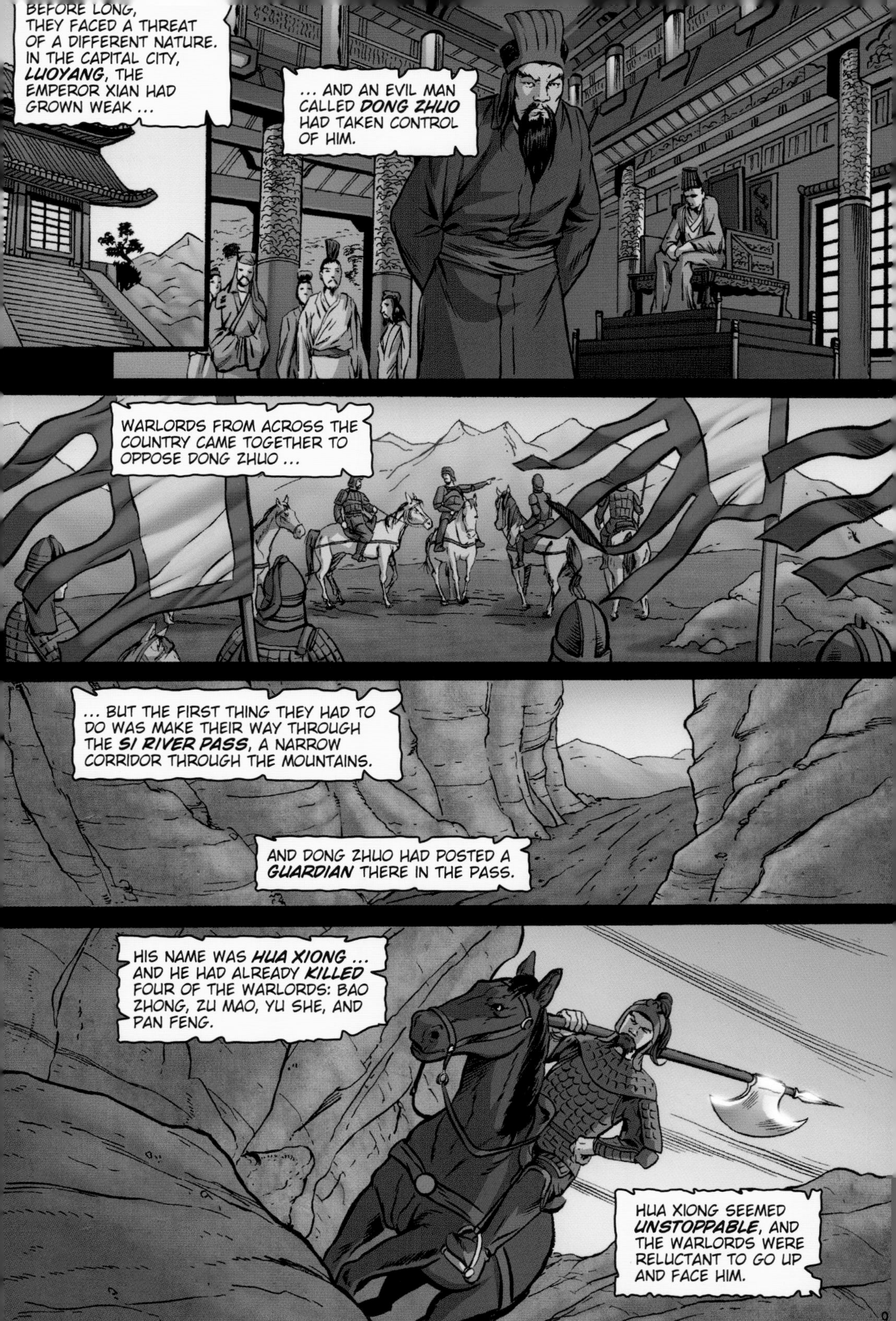
BEFORE LONG, THEY FACED A THREAT OF A DIFFERENT NATURE. IN THE CAPITAL CITY, LUOYANG, THE EMPEROR XIAN HAD GROWN WEAK ...
... AND AN EVIL MAN CALLED DONG ZHUO HAD TAKEN CONTROL OF HIM.
WARLORDS FROM ACROSS THE COUNTRY CAME TOGETHER TO OPPOSE DONG ZHUO ...
... BUT THE FIRST THING THEY HAD TO DO WAS MAKE THEIR WAY THROUGH THE SI RIVER PASS, A NARROW CORRIDOR THROUGH THE MOUNTAINS.
AND DONG ZHUO HAD POSTED A GUARDIAN THERE IN THE PASS.
HIS NAME WAS HUA XIONG ... AND HE HAD ALREADY KILLED FOUR OF THE WARLORDS: BAO ZHONG, ZU MAO, YU SHE, AND PAN FENG.
HUA XIONG SEEMED UNSTOPPABLE, AND THE WARLORDS WERE RELUCTANT TO GO UP AND FACE HIM.

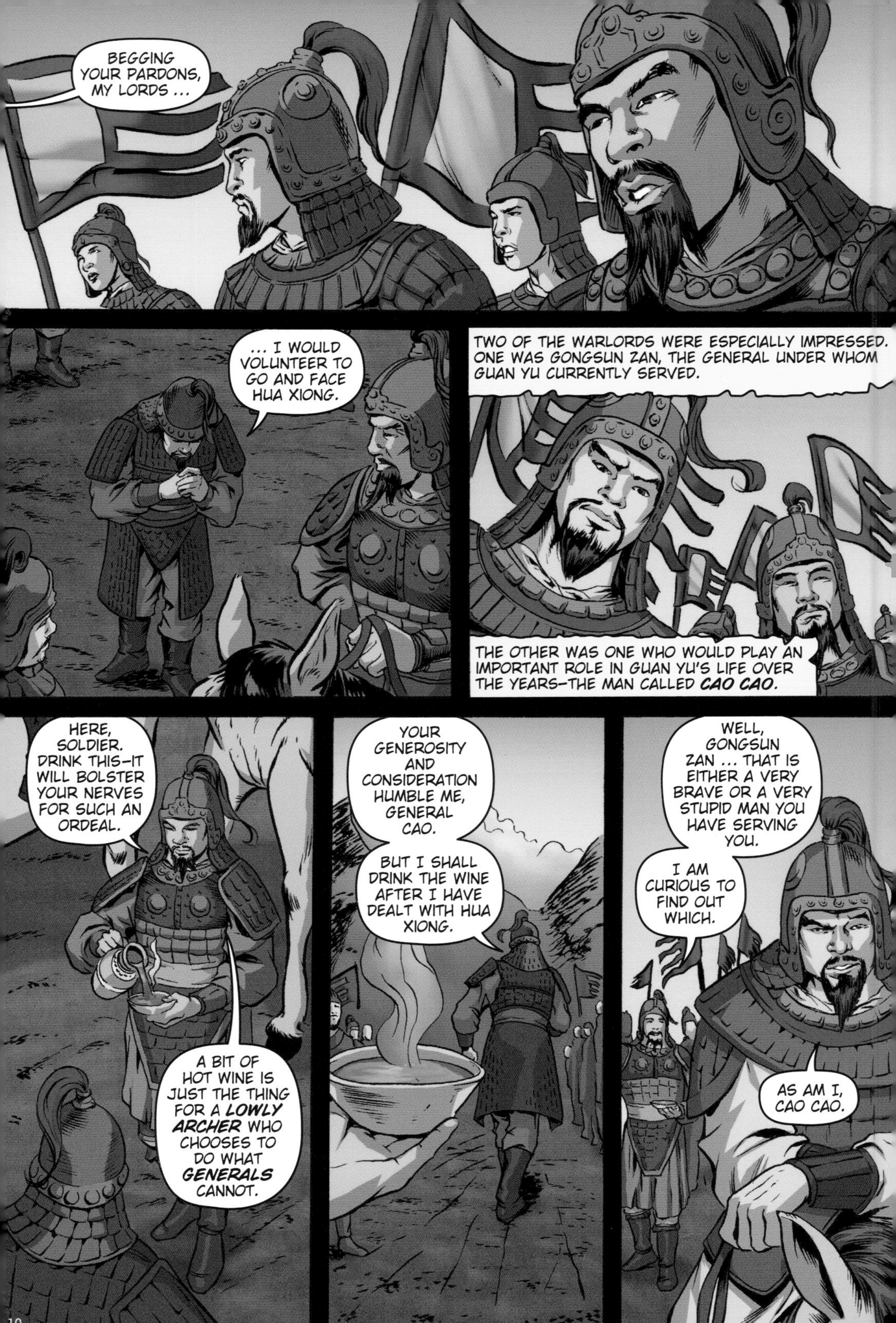
BEGGING YOUR PARDONS, MY LORDS ...
... I WOULD VOLUNTEER TO GO AND FACE HUA XIONG.
TWO OF THE WARLORDS WERE ESPECIALLY IMPRESSED. ONE WAS GONGSUN ZAN, THE GENERAL UNDER WHOM GUAN YU CURRENTLY SERVED.
THE OTHER WAS ONE WHO WOULD PLAY AN IMPORTANT ROLE IN GUAN YU'S LIFE OVER THE YEARS–THE MAN CALLED ***CAO CAO***.
HERE, SOLDIER. DRINK THIS–IT WILL BOLSTER YOUR NERVES FOR SUCH AN ORDEAL.
A BIT OF HOT WINE IS JUST THE THING FOR A ***LOWLY ARCHER*** WHO CHOOSES TO DO WHAT ***GENERALS*** CANNOT.
YOUR GENEROSITY AND CONSIDERATION HUMBLE ME, GENERAL CAO.
BUT I SHALL DRINK THE WINE AFTER I HAVE DEALT WITH HUA XIONG.
WELL, GONGSUN ZAN ... THAT IS EITHER A VERY BRAVE OR A VERY STUPID MAN YOU HAVE SERVING YOU.
I AM CURIOUS TO FIND OUT WHICH.
AS AM I, CAO CAO.

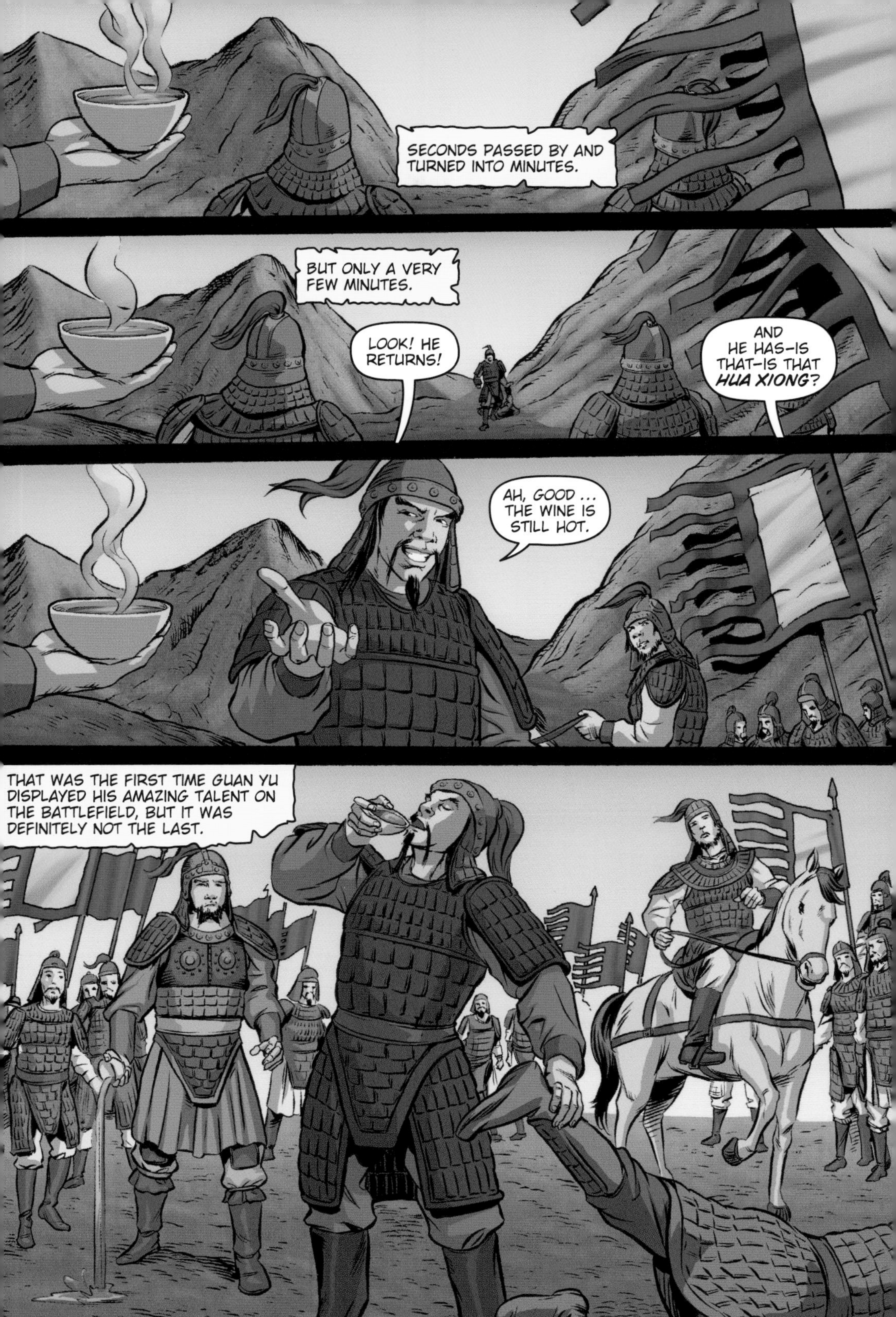
SECONDS PASSED BY AND TURNED INTO MINUTES.
BUT ONLY A VERY FEW MINUTES.
LOOK! HE RETURNS!
AND HE HAS–IS THAT–IS THAT *HUA XIONG*?
AH, GOOD ... THE WINE IS STILL HOT.
THAT WAS THE FIRST TIME GUAN YU DISPLAYED HIS AMAZING TALENT ON THE BATTLEFIELD, BUT IT WAS DEFINITELY NOT THE LAST.

BLOOD BROTHERS UNITED

GUAN YU AND ZHANG FEI FOUGHT FOR LIU BEI IN MANY BATTLES, PROVING THEMSELVES TO BE FEARSOME WARRIORS.

SOON LIU BEI BECAME GOVERNOR OF PINGYUAN COUNTY. QUICKLY HE PROMOTED GUAN YU AND ZHANG FEI TO COMMANDERS.

NO MATTER HOW DANGEROUS THINGS BECAME, GUAN YU AND ZHANG FEI STUCK WITH LIU BEI.

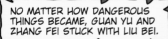

THEY HAD SWORN TO FOLLOW HIM UNQUESTIONINGLY AND TO PROTECT HIM FROM EVERY THREAT.

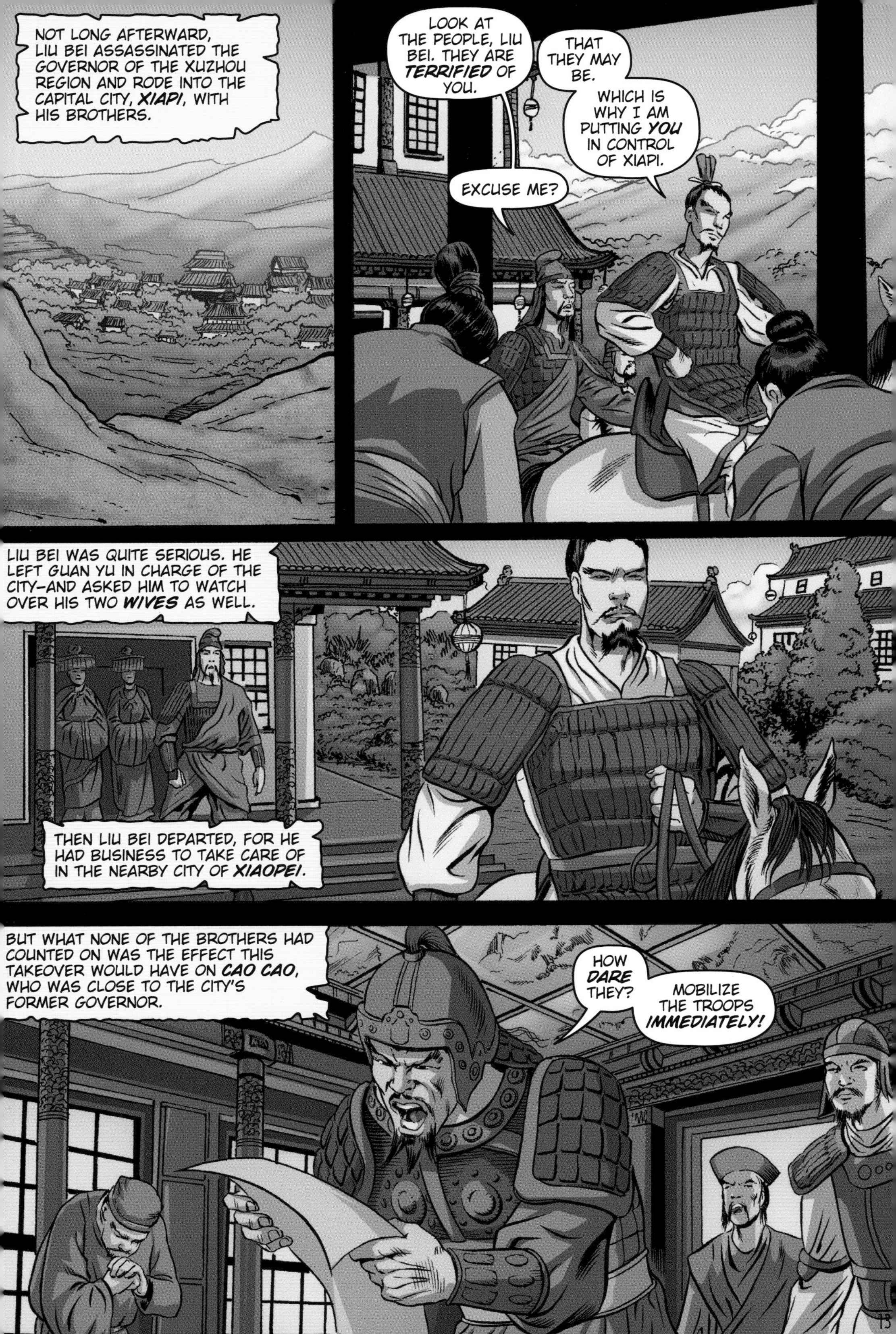
NOT LONG AFTERWARD, LIU BEI ASSASSINATED THE GOVERNOR OF THE XUZHOU REGION AND RODE INTO THE CAPITAL CITY, ***XIAPI***, WITH HIS BROTHERS.
LOOK AT THE PEOPLE, LIU BEI. THEY ARE ***TERRIFIED*** OF YOU.
THAT THEY MAY BE.
WHICH IS WHY I AM PUTTING ***YOU*** IN CONTROL OF XIAPI.
EXCUSE ME?
LIU BEI WAS QUITE SERIOUS. HE LEFT GUAN YU IN CHARGE OF THE CITY—AND ASKED HIM TO WATCH OVER HIS TWO ***WIVES*** AS WELL.
THEN LIU BEI DEPARTED, FOR HE HAD BUSINESS TO TAKE CARE OF IN THE NEARBY CITY OF ***XIAOPEI***.
BUT WHAT NONE OF THE BROTHERS HAD COUNTED ON WAS THE EFFECT THIS TAKEOVER WOULD HAVE ON ***CAO CAO***, WHO WAS CLOSE TO THE CITY'S FORMER GOVERNOR.
HOW ***DARE*** THEY?
MOBILIZE THE TROOPS ***IMMEDIATELY!***

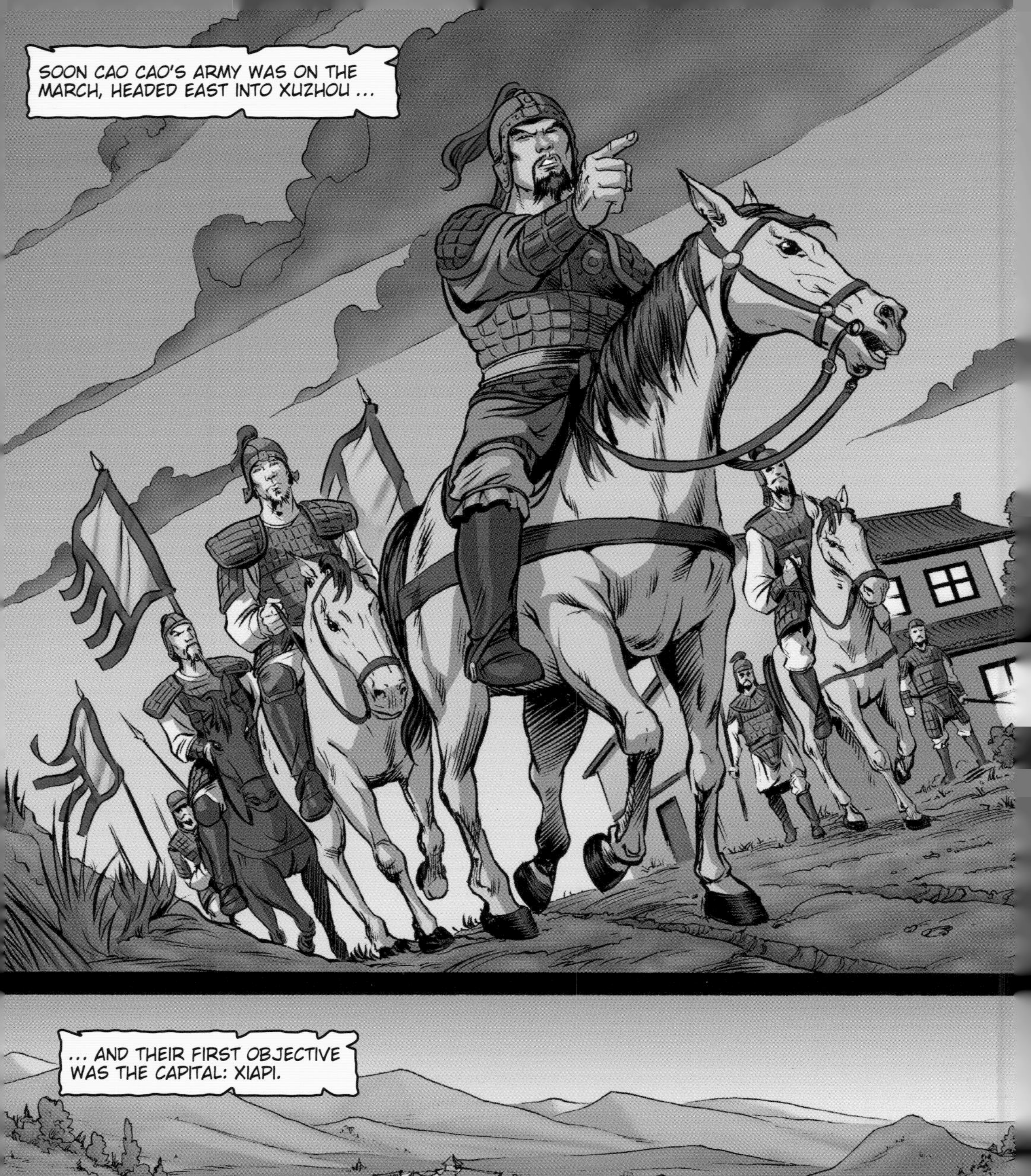
SOON CAO CAO'S ARMY WAS ON THE MARCH, HEADED EAST INTO XUZHOU ...

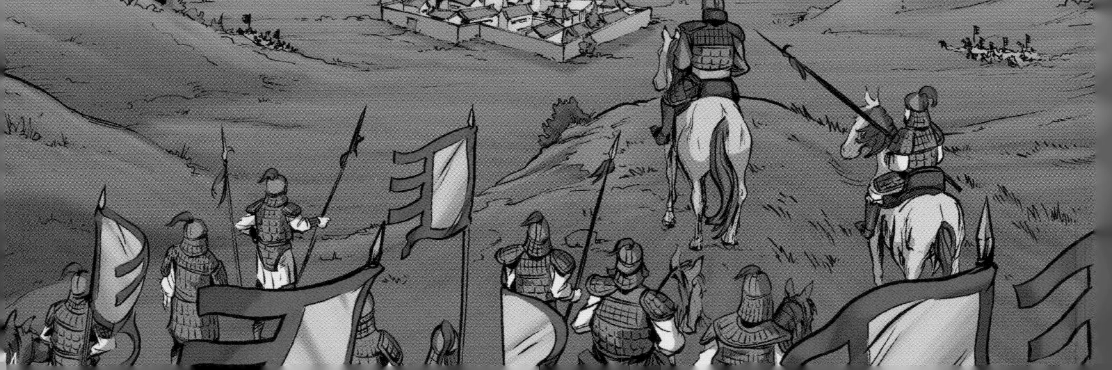
... AND THEIR FIRST OBJECTIVE WAS THE CAPITAL: XIAPI.

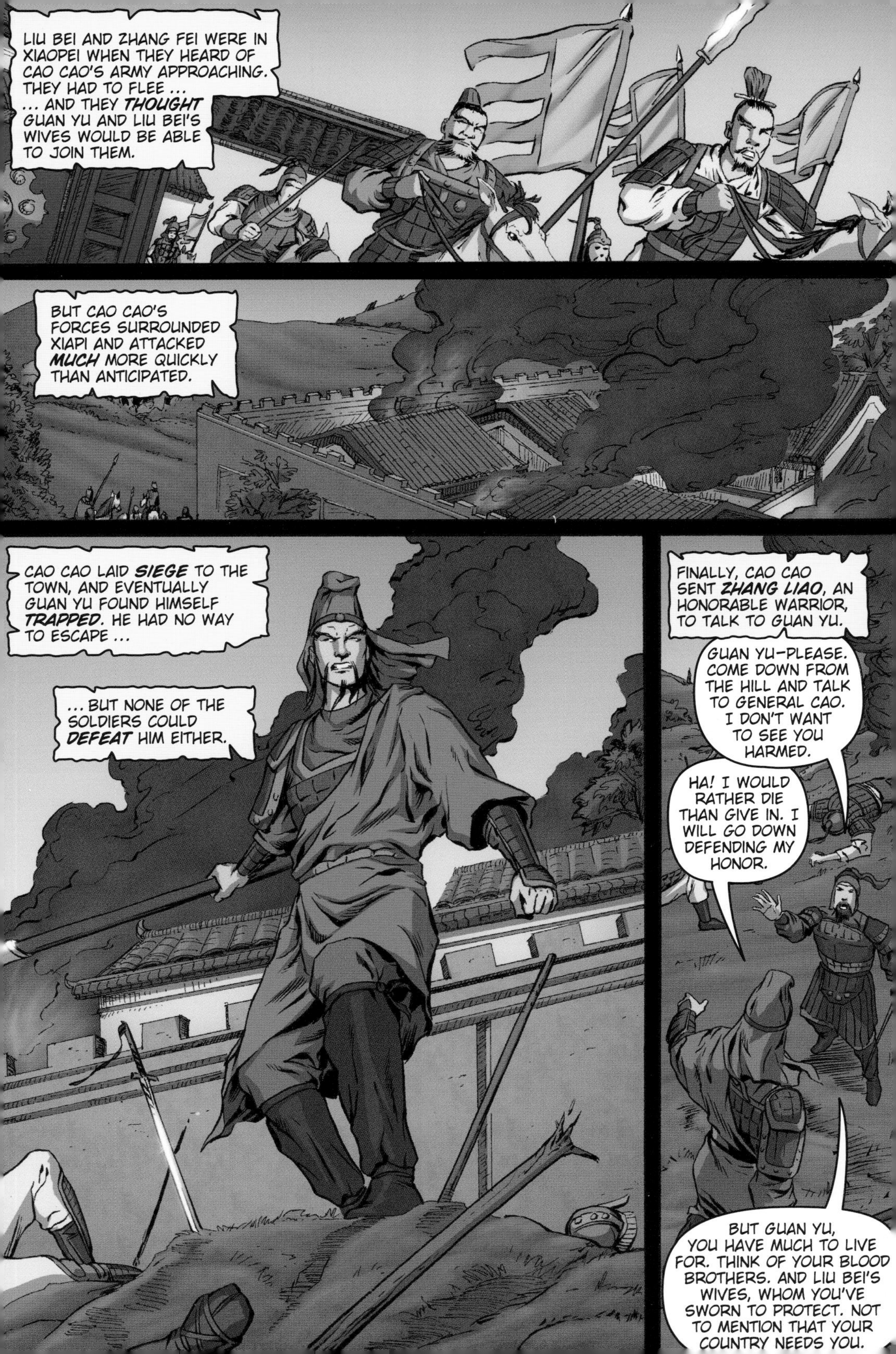
LIU BEI AND ZHANG FEI WERE IN XIAOPEI WHEN THEY HEARD OF CAO CAO'S ARMY APPROACHING. THEY HAD TO FLEE ...
... AND THEY *THOUGHT* GUAN YU AND LIU BEI'S WIVES WOULD BE ABLE TO JOIN THEM.
BUT CAO CAO'S FORCES SURROUNDED XIAPI AND ATTACKED *MUCH* MORE QUICKLY THAN ANTICIPATED.
CAO CAO LAID *SIEGE* TO THE TOWN, AND EVENTUALLY GUAN YU FOUND HIMSELF *TRAPPED*. HE HAD NO WAY TO ESCAPE ...
... BUT NONE OF THE SOLDIERS COULD *DEFEAT* HIM EITHER.
FINALLY, CAO CAO SENT *ZHANG LIAO*, AN HONORABLE WARRIOR, TO TALK TO GUAN YU.
GUAN YU–PLEASE. COME DOWN FROM THE HILL AND TALK TO GENERAL CAO. I DON'T WANT TO SEE YOU HARMED.
HA! I WOULD RATHER DIE THAN GIVE IN. I WILL GO DOWN DEFENDING MY HONOR.
BUT GUAN YU, YOU HAVE MUCH TO LIVE FOR. THINK OF YOUR BLOOD BROTHERS. AND LIU BEI'S WIVES, WHOM YOU'VE SWORN TO PROTECT. NOT TO MENTION THAT YOUR COUNTRY NEEDS YOU.

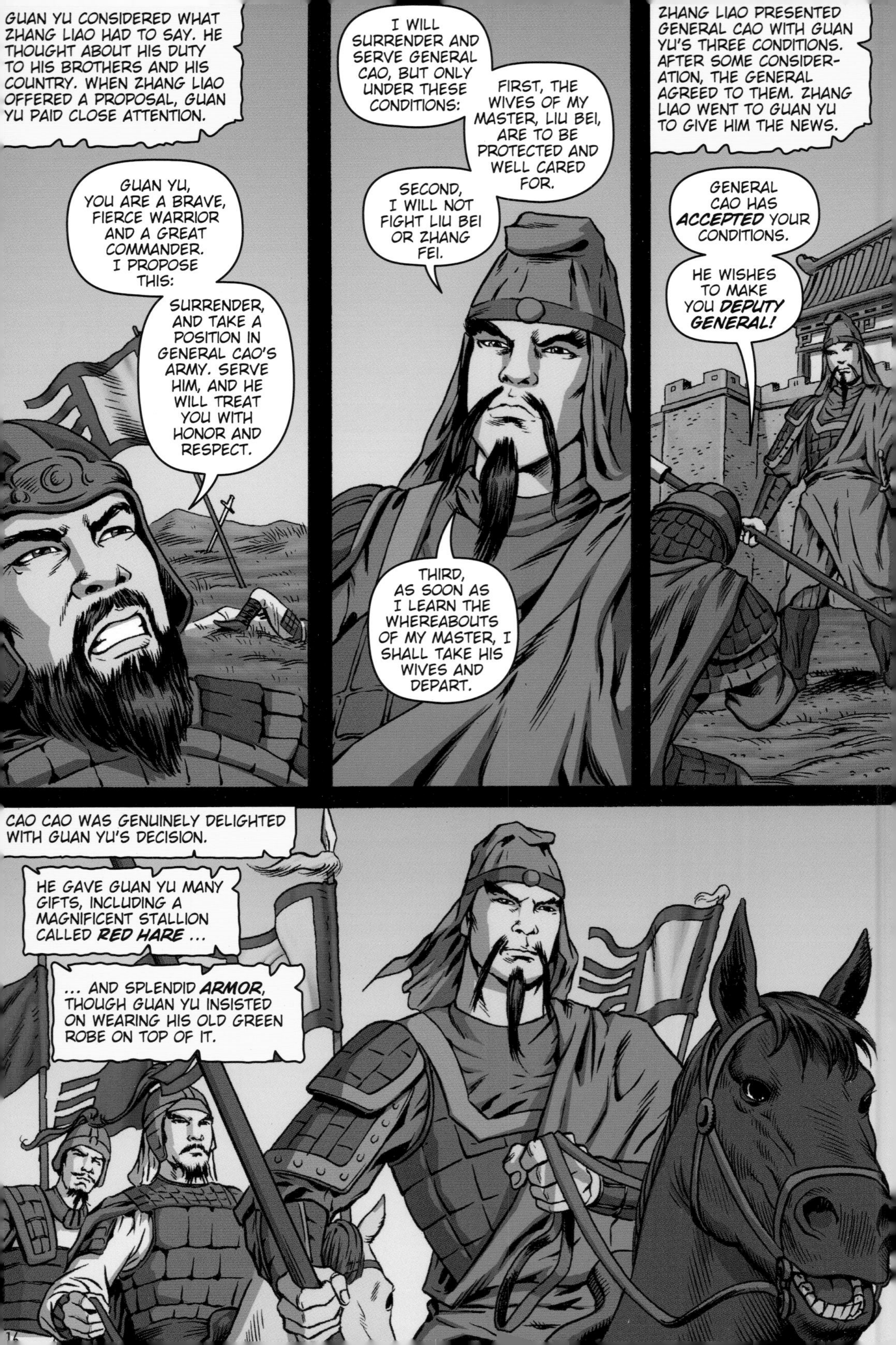
GUAN YU CONSIDERED WHAT ZHANG LIAO HAD TO SAY. HE THOUGHT ABOUT HIS DUTY TO HIS BROTHERS AND HIS COUNTRY. WHEN ZHANG LIAO OFFERED A PROPOSAL, GUAN YU PAID CLOSE ATTENTION.
GUAN YU, YOU ARE A BRAVE, FIERCE WARRIOR AND A GREAT COMMANDER. I PROPOSE THIS:
SURRENDER, AND TAKE A POSITION IN GENERAL CAO'S ARMY. SERVE HIM, AND HE WILL TREAT YOU WITH HONOR AND RESPECT.
I WILL SURRENDER AND SERVE GENERAL CAO, BUT ONLY UNDER THESE CONDITIONS:
FIRST, THE WIVES OF MY MASTER, LIU BEI, ARE TO BE PROTECTED AND WELL CARED FOR.
SECOND, I WILL NOT FIGHT LIU BEI OR ZHANG FEI.
THIRD, AS SOON AS I LEARN THE WHEREABOUTS OF MY MASTER, I SHALL TAKE HIS WIVES AND DEPART.
ZHANG LIAO PRESENTED GENERAL CAO WITH GUAN YU'S THREE CONDITIONS. AFTER SOME CONSIDERATION, THE GENERAL AGREED TO THEM. ZHANG LIAO WENT TO GUAN YU TO GIVE HIM THE NEWS.
GENERAL CAO HAS ***ACCEPTED*** YOUR CONDITIONS.
HE WISHES TO MAKE YOU ***DEPUTY GENERAL!***
CAO CAO WAS GENUINELY DELIGHTED WITH GUAN YU'S DECISION.
HE GAVE GUAN YU MANY GIFTS, INCLUDING A MAGNIFICENT STALLION CALLED ***RED HARE*** ...
... AND SPLENDID ***ARMOR***, THOUGH GUAN YU INSISTED ON WEARING HIS OLD GREEN ROBE ON TOP OF IT.

A NEW ALLEGIANCE

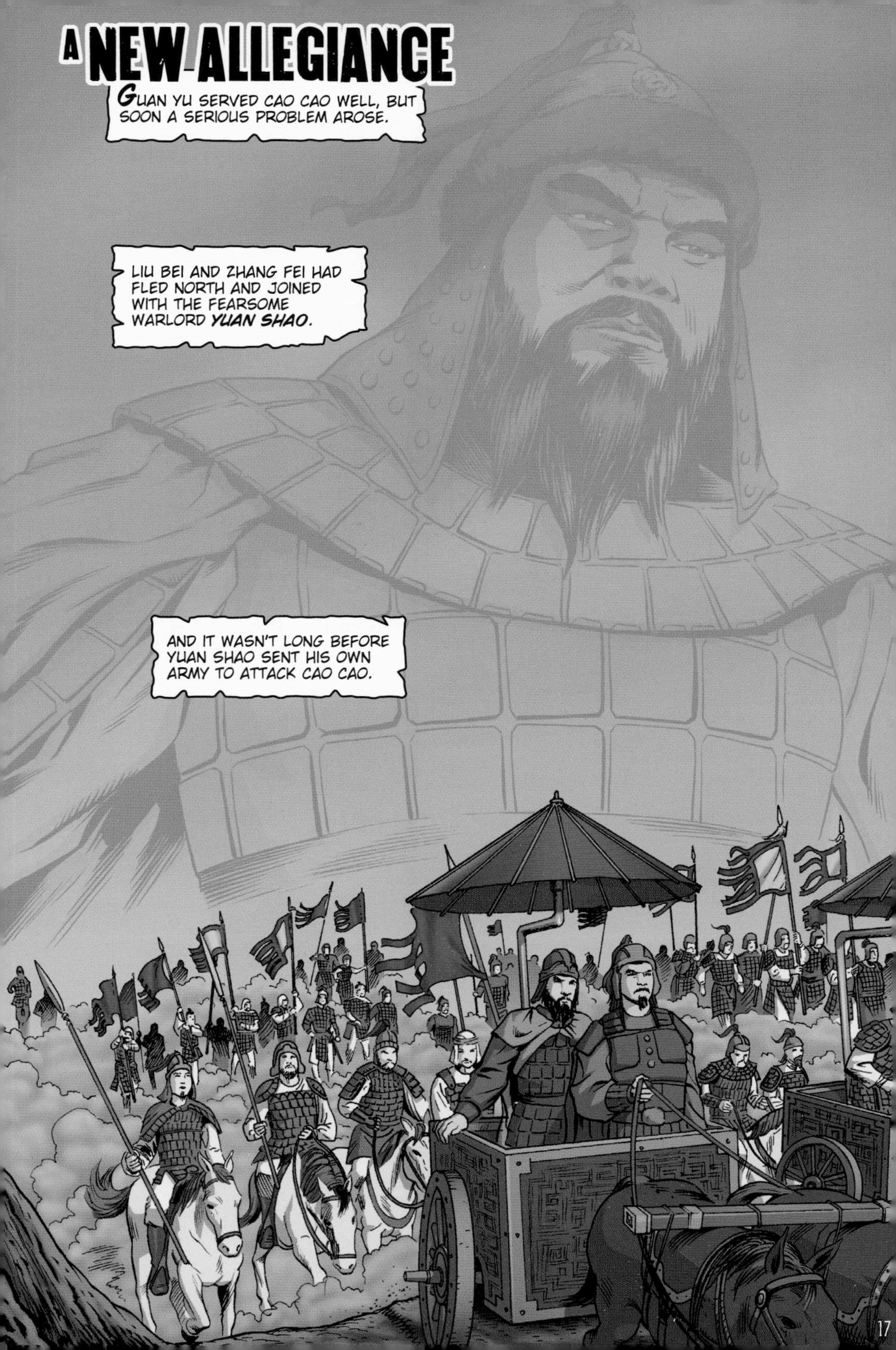
GUAN YU SERVED CAO CAO WELL, BUT SOON A SERIOUS PROBLEM AROSE.
LIU BEI AND ZHANG FEI HAD FLED NORTH AND JOINED WITH THE FEARSOME WARLORD YUAN SHAO.
AND IT WASN'T LONG BEFORE YUAN SHAO SENT HIS OWN ARMY TO ATTACK CAO CAO.

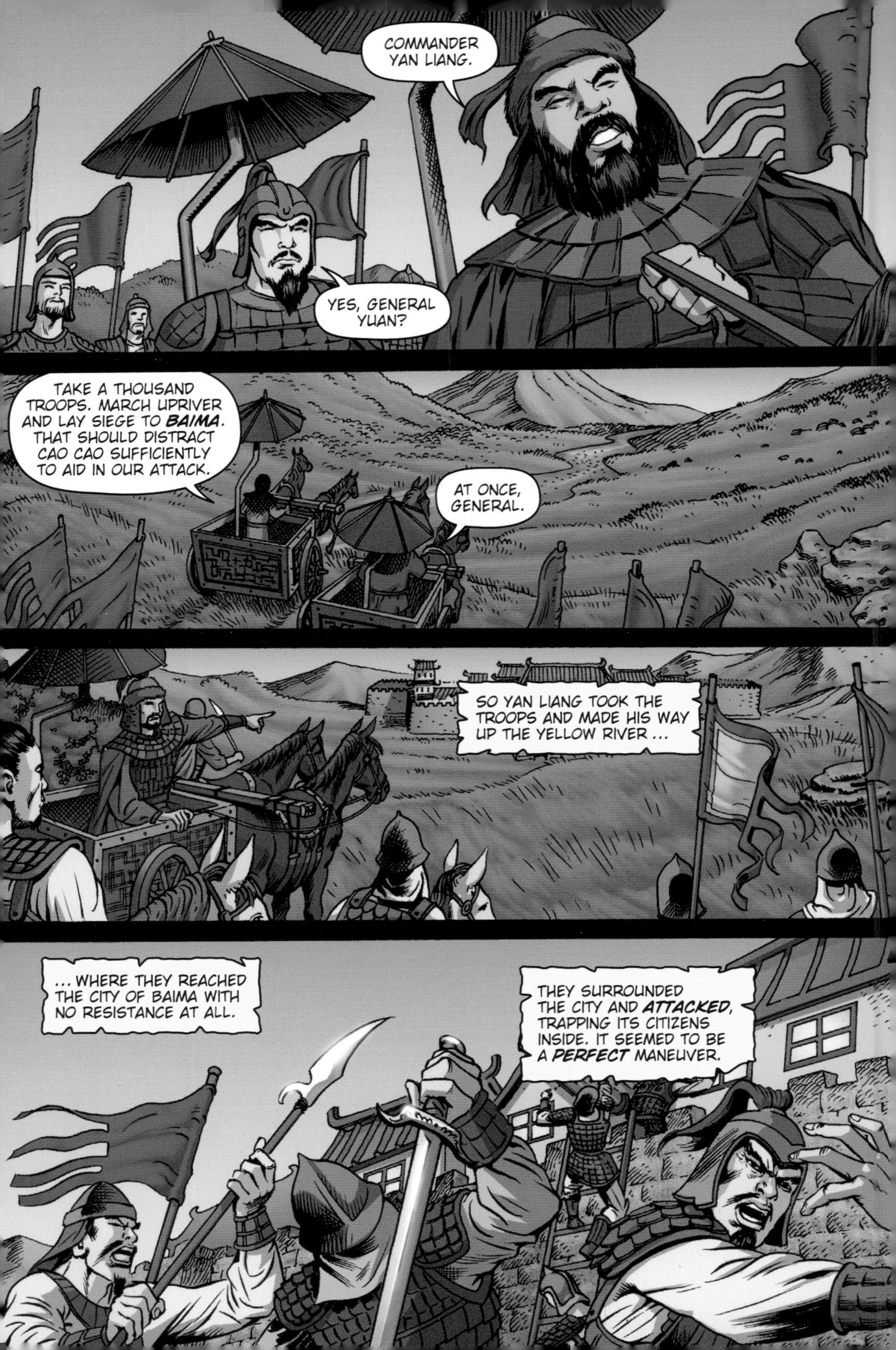
COMMANDER YAN LIANG.
YES, GENERAL YUAN?
TAKE A THOUSAND TROOPS. MARCH UPRIVER AND LAY SIEGE TO **BAIMA**. THAT SHOULD DISTRACT CAO CAO SUFFICIENTLY TO AID IN OUR ATTACK.
AT ONCE, GENERAL.
SO YAN LIANG TOOK THE TROOPS AND MADE HIS WAY UP THE YELLOW RIVER ...
... WHERE THEY REACHED THE CITY OF BAIMA WITH NO RESISTANCE AT ALL.
THEY SURROUNDED THE CITY AND **ATTACKED**, TRAPPING ITS CITIZENS INSIDE. IT SEEMED TO BE A **PERFECT** MANEUVER.

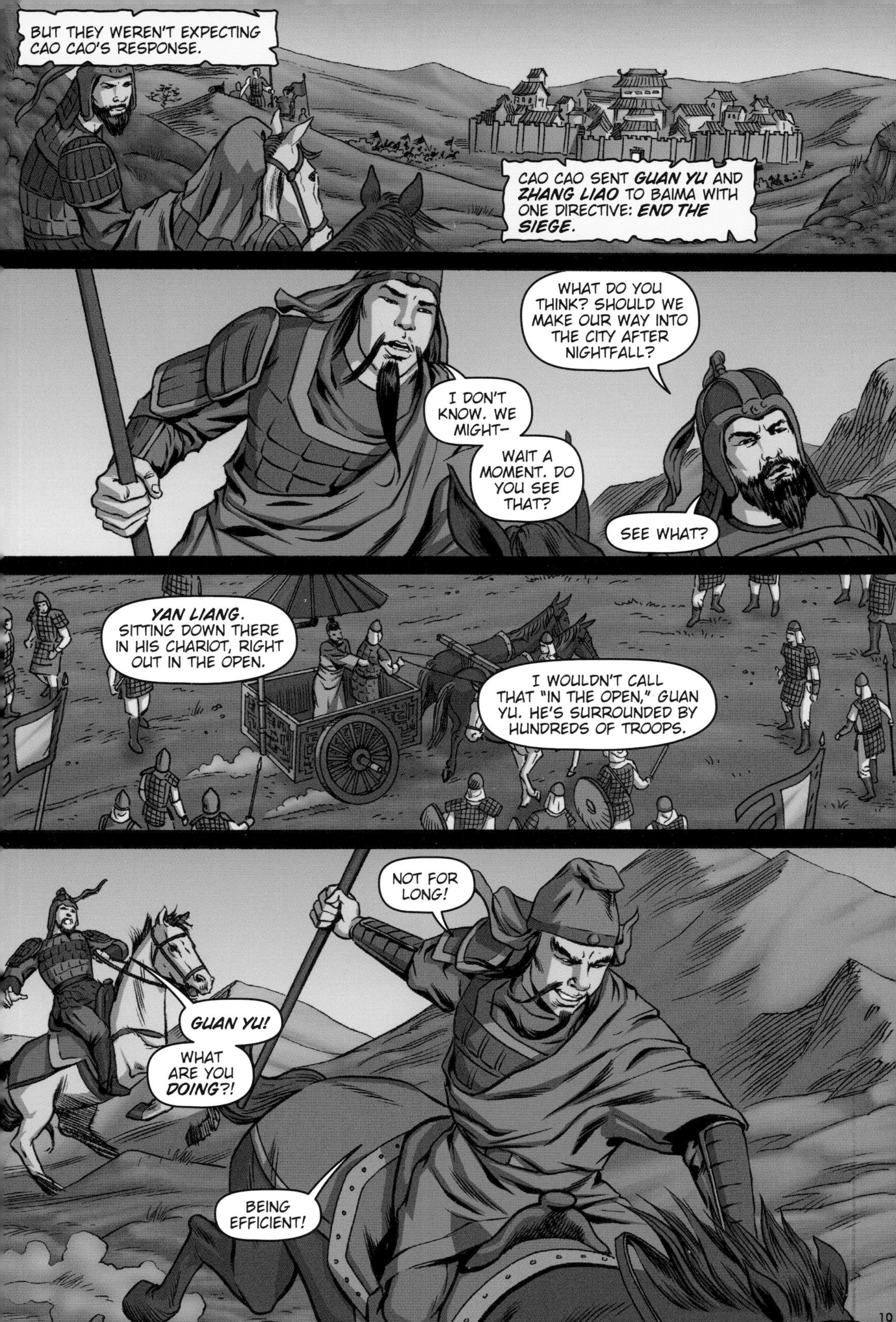

BUT THEY WEREN'T EXPECTING CAO CAO'S RESPONSE.
CAO CAO SENT GUAN YU AND ZHANG LIAO TO BAIMA WITH ONE DIRECTIVE: END THE SIEGE.
WHAT DO YOU THINK? SHOULD WE MAKE OUR WAY INTO THE CITY AFTER NIGHTFALL?
I DON'T KNOW. WE MIGHT–
WAIT A MOMENT. DO YOU SEE THAT?
SEE WHAT?
YAN LIANG. SITTING DOWN THERE IN HIS CHARIOT, RIGHT OUT IN THE OPEN.
I WOULDN'T CALL THAT "IN THE OPEN," GUAN YU. HE'S SURROUNDED BY HUNDREDS OF TROOPS.
NOT FOR LONG!
GUAN YU!
WHAT ARE YOU DOING?!
BEING EFFICIENT!

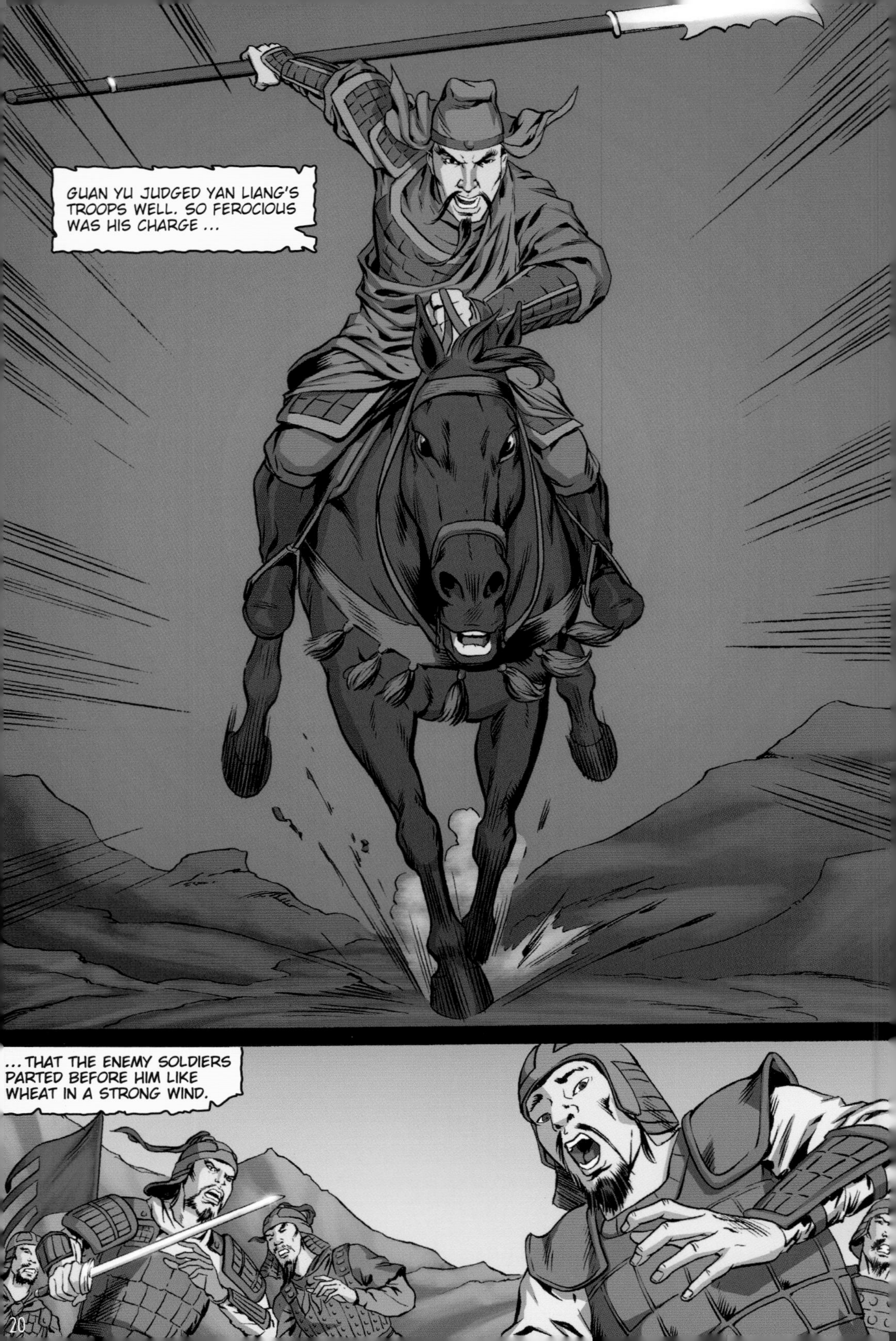
GUAN YU JUDGED YAN LIANG'S TROOPS WELL. SO FEROCIOUS WAS HIS CHARGE ...
... THAT THE ENEMY SOLDIERS PARTED BEFORE HIM LIKE WHEAT IN A STRONG WIND.

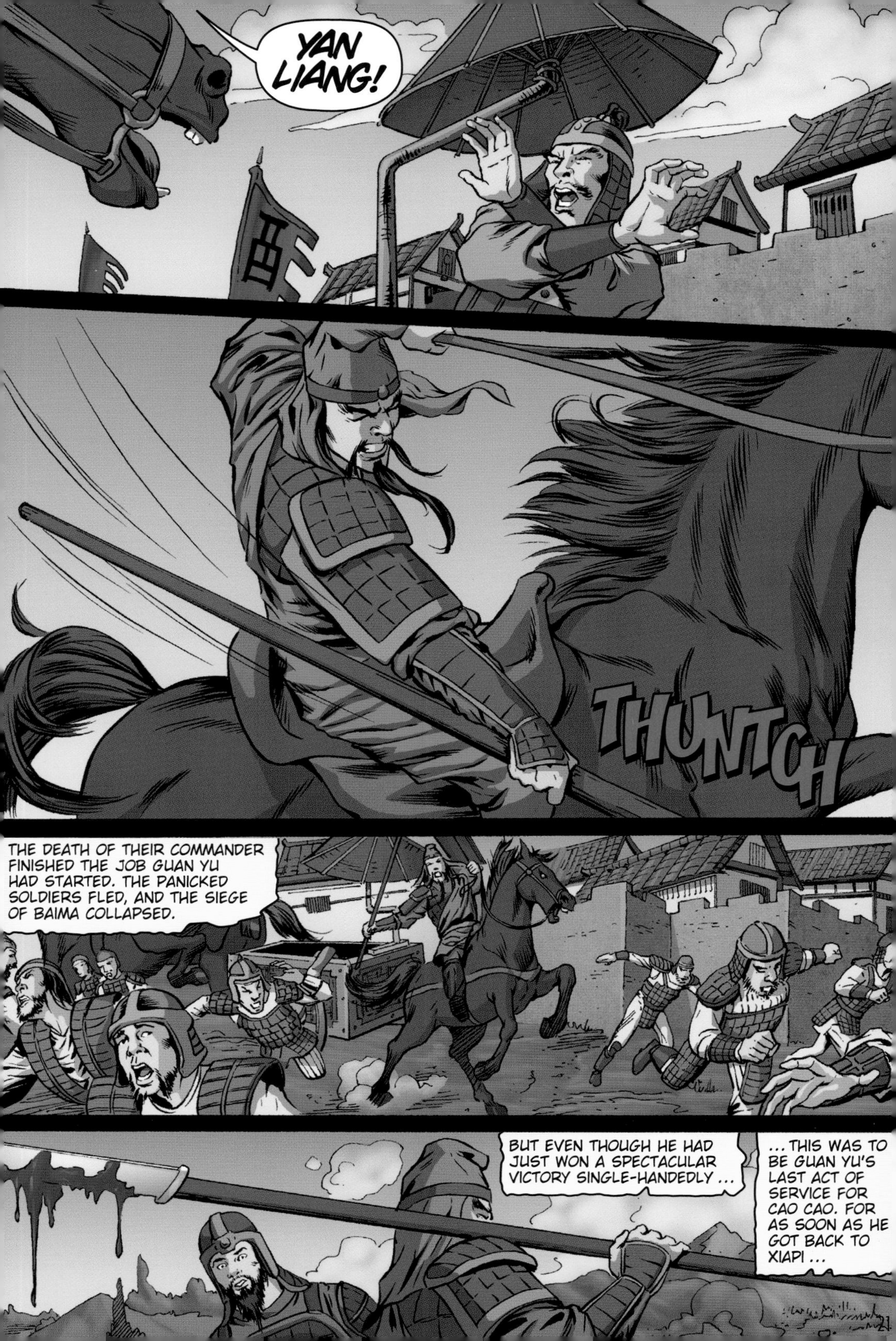

YAN LIANG!
THUNTCH
THE DEATH OF THEIR COMMANDER FINISHED THE JOB GUAN YU HAD STARTED. THE PANICKED SOLDIERS FLED, AND THE SIEGE OF BAIMA COLLAPSED.
BUT EVEN THOUGH HE HAD JUST WON A SPECTACULAR VICTORY SINGLE-HANDEDLY ...
... THIS WAS TO BE GUAN YU'S LAST ACT OF SERVICE FOR CAO CAO. FOR AS SOON AS HE GOT BACK TO XIAPI ...

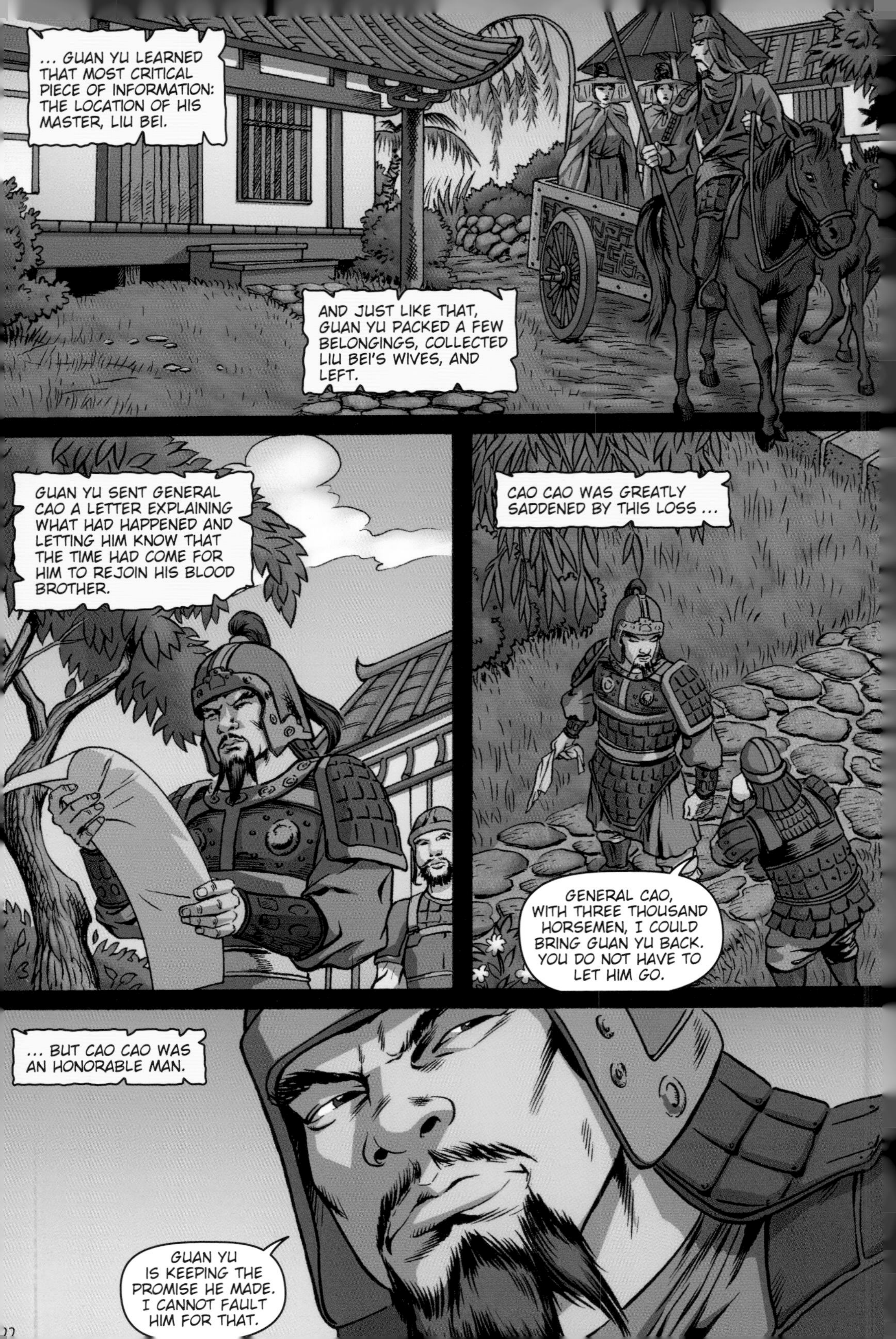
... GUAN YU LEARNED THAT MOST CRITICAL PIECE OF INFORMATION: THE LOCATION OF HIS MASTER, LIU BEI.
AND JUST LIKE THAT, GUAN YU PACKED A FEW BELONGINGS, COLLECTED LIU BEI'S WIVES, AND LEFT.
GUAN YU SENT GENERAL CAO A LETTER EXPLAINING WHAT HAD HAPPENED AND LETTING HIM KNOW THAT THE TIME HAD COME FOR HIM TO REJOIN HIS BLOOD BROTHER.
CAO CAO WAS GREATLY SADDENED BY THIS LOSS ...
GENERAL CAO, WITH THREE THOUSAND HORSEMEN, I COULD BRING GUAN YU BACK. YOU DO NOT HAVE TO LET HIM GO.
... BUT CAO CAO WAS AN HONORABLE MAN.
GUAN YU IS KEEPING THE PROMISE HE MADE. I CANNOT FAULT HIM FOR THAT.

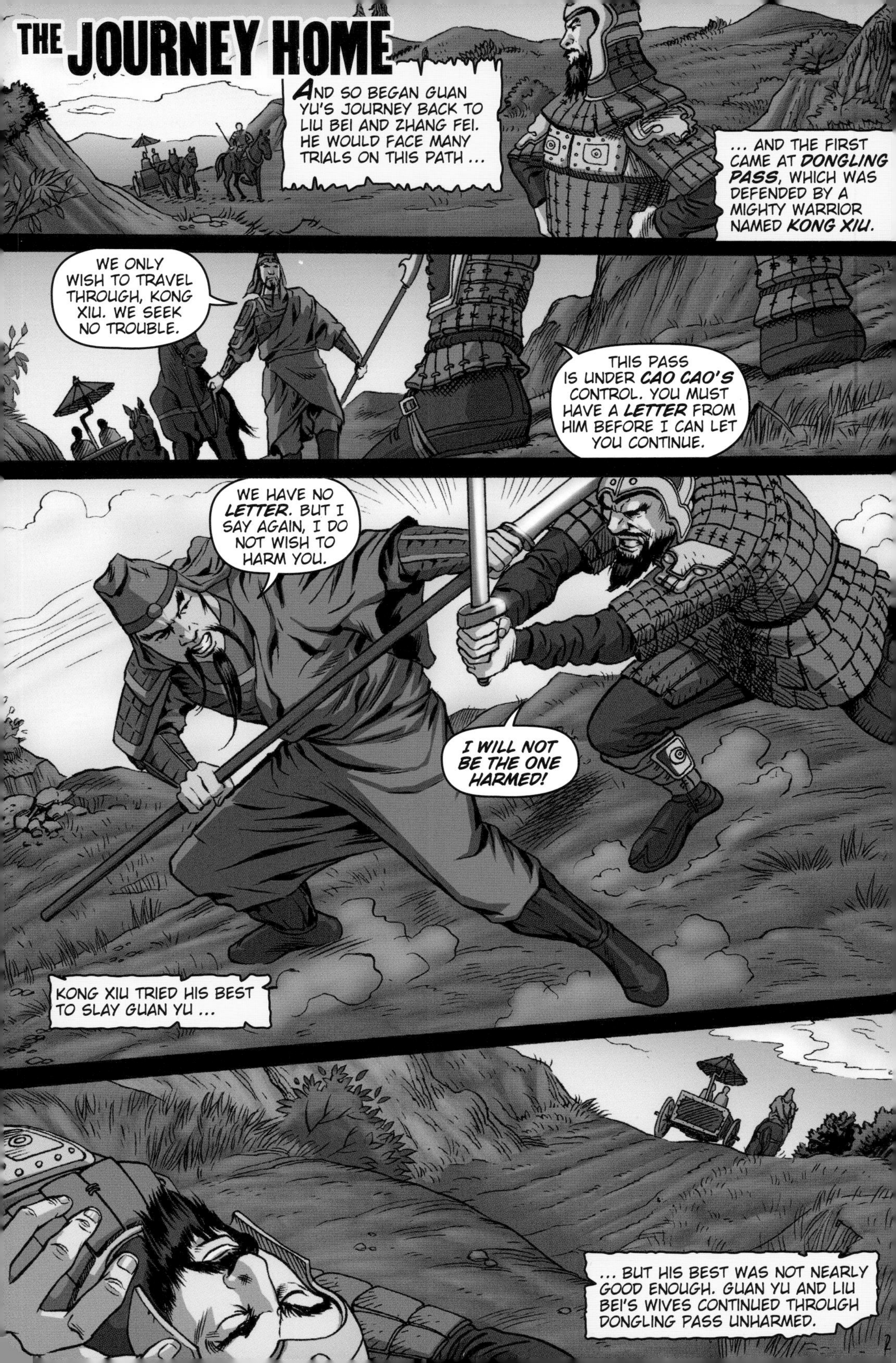
THE JOURNEY HOME
AND SO BEGAN GUAN YU'S JOURNEY BACK TO LIU BEI AND ZHANG FEI. HE WOULD FACE MANY TRIALS ON THIS PATH ...
... AND THE FIRST CAME AT DONGLING PASS, WHICH WAS DEFENDED BY A MIGHTY WARRIOR NAMED KONG XIU.
WE ONLY WISH TO TRAVEL THROUGH, KONG XIU. WE SEEK NO TROUBLE.
THIS PASS IS UNDER CAO CAO'S CONTROL. YOU MUST HAVE A LETTER FROM HIM BEFORE I CAN LET YOU CONTINUE.
WE HAVE NO LETTER. BUT I SAY AGAIN, I DO NOT WISH TO HARM YOU.
I WILL NOT BE THE ONE HARMED!
KONG XIU TRIED HIS BEST TO SLAY GUAN YU ...
... BUT HIS BEST WAS NOT NEARLY GOOD ENOUGH. GUAN YU AND LIU BEI'S WIVES CONTINUED THROUGH DONGLING PASS UNHARMED.

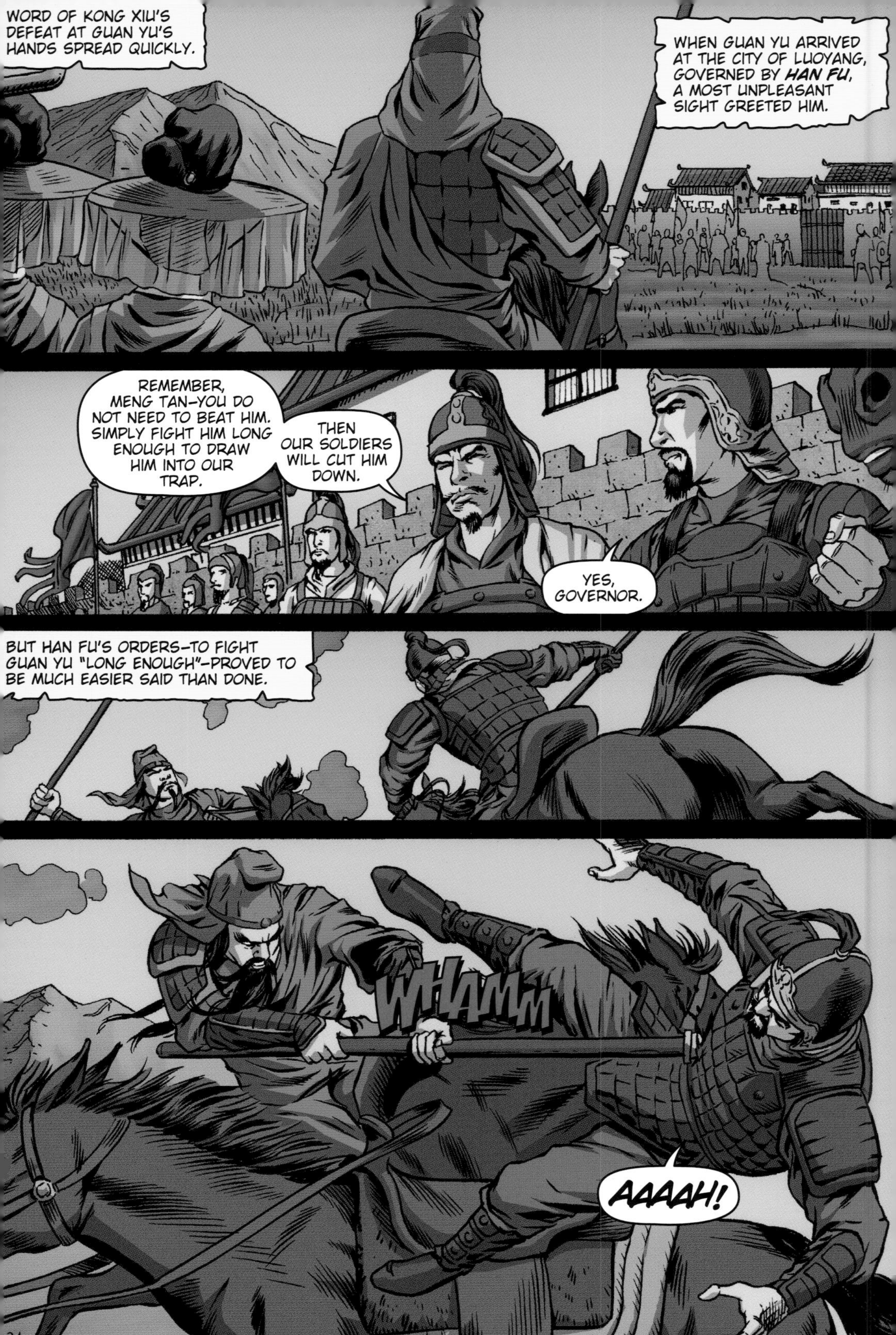
WORD OF KONG XIU'S DEFEAT AT GUAN YU'S HANDS SPREAD QUICKLY.
WHEN GUAN YU ARRIVED AT THE CITY OF LUOYANG, GOVERNED BY HAN FU, A MOST UNPLEASANT SIGHT GREETED HIM.
REMEMBER, MENG TAN–YOU DO NOT NEED TO BEAT HIM. SIMPLY FIGHT HIM LONG ENOUGH TO DRAW HIM INTO OUR TRAP.
THEN OUR SOLDIERS WILL CUT HIM DOWN.
YES, GOVERNOR.
BUT HAN FU'S ORDERS–TO FIGHT GUAN YU "LONG ENOUGH"–PROVED TO BE MUCH EASIER SAID THAN DONE.
WHAMM
AAAAH!

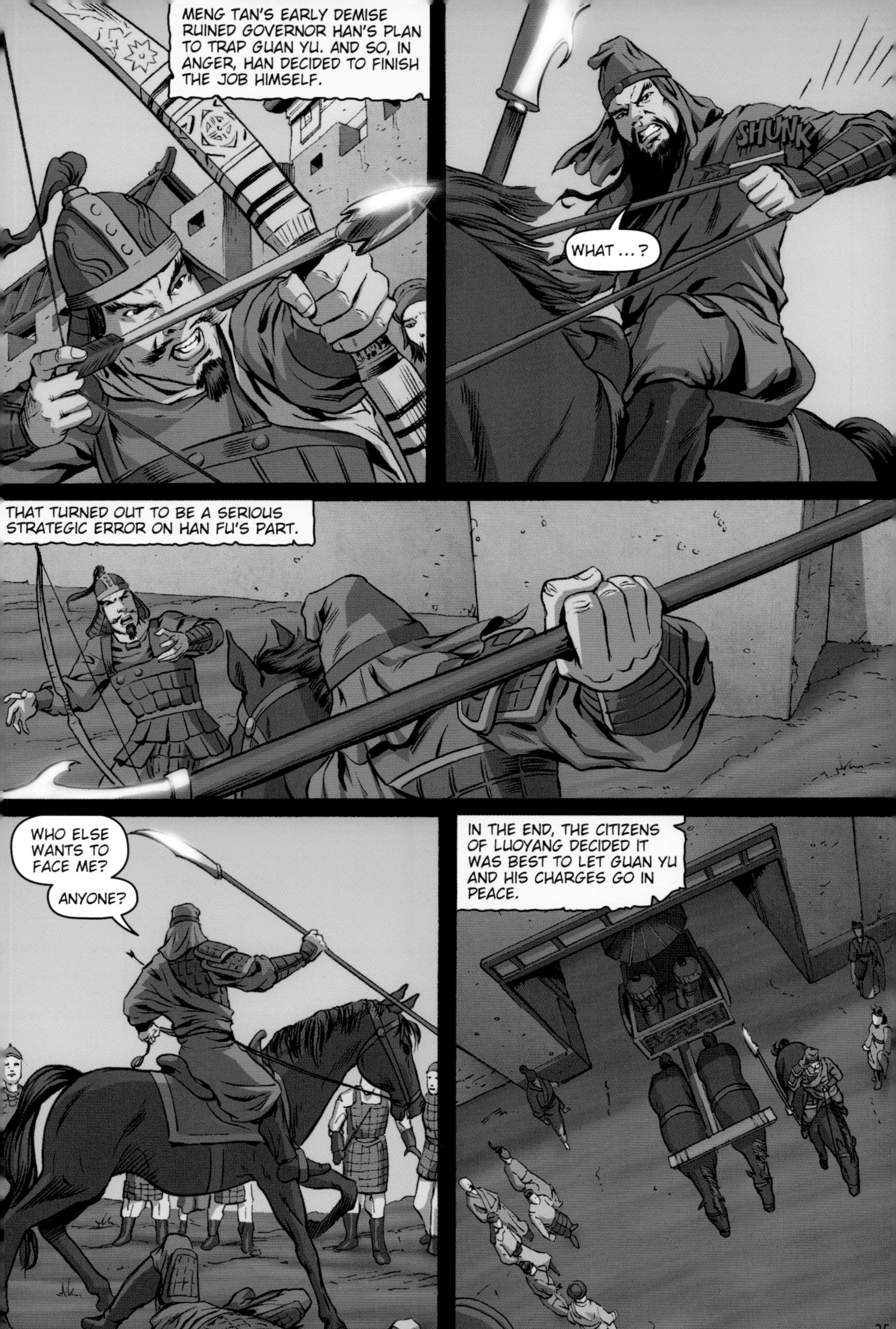
MENG TAN'S EARLY DEMISE RUINED GOVERNOR HAN'S PLAN TO TRAP GUAN YU. AND SO, IN ANGER, HAN DECIDED TO FINISH THE JOB HIMSELF.
SHUNK
WHAT ...?
THAT TURNED OUT TO BE A SERIOUS STRATEGIC ERROR ON HAN FU'S PART.
WHO ELSE WANTS TO FACE ME?
ANYONE?
IN THE END, THE CITIZENS OF LUOYANG DECIDED IT WAS BEST TO LET GUAN YU AND HIS CHARGES GO IN PEACE.

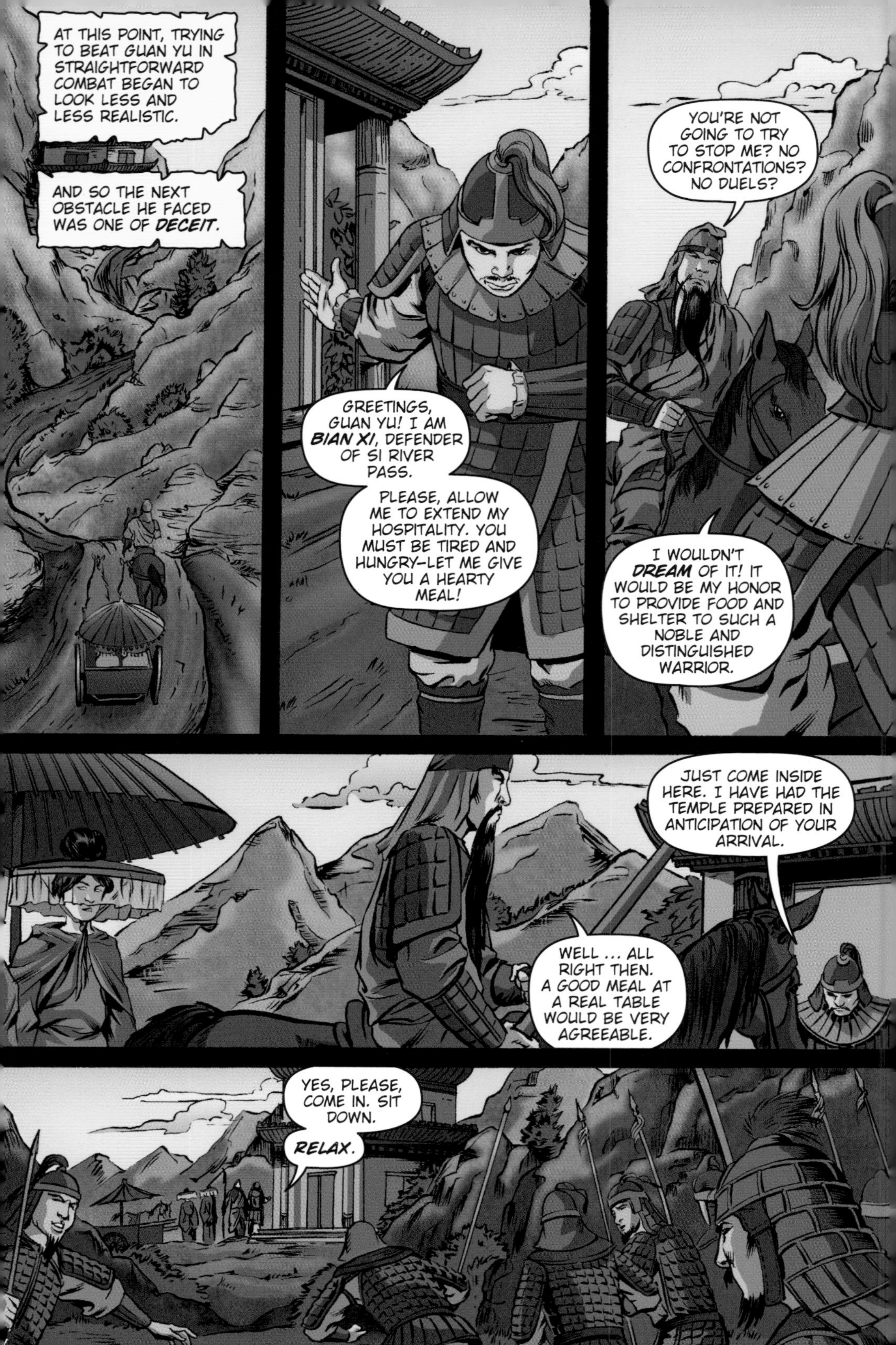
AT THIS POINT, TRYING TO BEAT GUAN YU IN STRAIGHTFORWARD COMBAT BEGAN TO LOOK LESS AND LESS REALISTIC.
AND SO THE NEXT OBSTACLE HE FACED WAS ONE OF DECEIT.
GREETINGS, GUAN YU! I AM BIAN XI, DEFENDER OF SI RIVER PASS.
PLEASE, ALLOW ME TO EXTEND MY HOSPITALITY. YOU MUST BE TIRED AND HUNGRY–LET ME GIVE YOU A HEARTY MEAL!
YOU'RE NOT GOING TO TRY TO STOP ME? NO CONFRONTATIONS? NO DUELS?
I WOULDN'T DREAM OF IT! IT WOULD BE MY HONOR TO PROVIDE FOOD AND SHELTER TO SUCH A NOBLE AND DISTINGUISHED WARRIOR.
JUST COME INSIDE HERE. I HAVE HAD THE TEMPLE PREPARED IN ANTICIPATION OF YOUR ARRIVAL.
WELL ... ALL RIGHT THEN. A GOOD MEAL AT A REAL TABLE WOULD BE VERY AGREEABLE.
YES, PLEASE, COME IN. SIT DOWN.
RELAX.

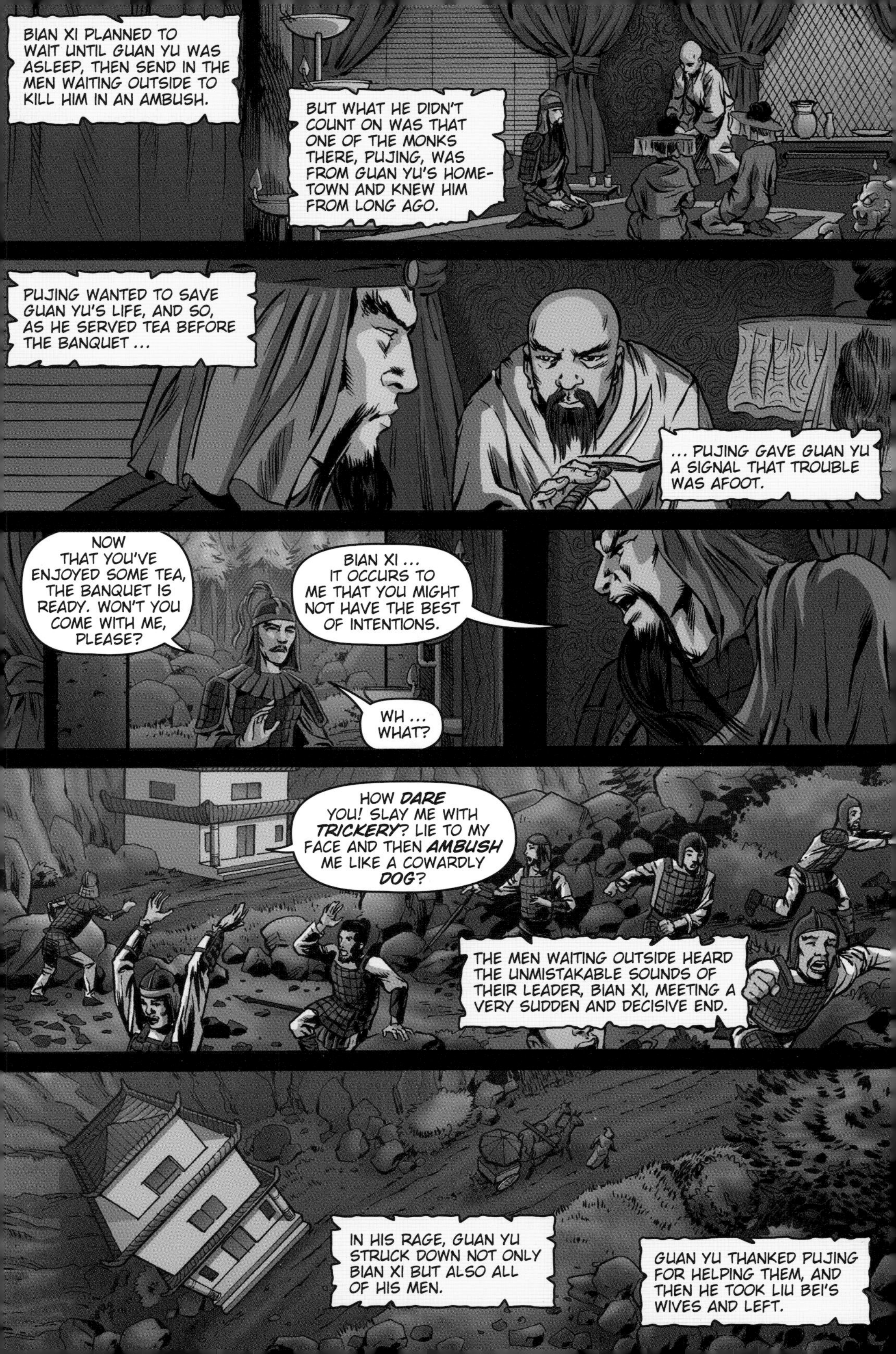
BIAN XI PLANNED TO WAIT UNTIL GUAN YU WAS ASLEEP, THEN SEND IN THE MEN WAITING OUTSIDE TO KILL HIM IN AN AMBUSH.
BUT WHAT HE DIDN'T COUNT ON WAS THAT ONE OF THE MONKS THERE, PUJING, WAS FROM GUAN YU'S HOME-TOWN AND KNEW HIM FROM LONG AGO.
PUJING WANTED TO SAVE GUAN YU'S LIFE, AND SO, AS HE SERVED TEA BEFORE THE BANQUET ...
... PUJING GAVE GUAN YU A SIGNAL THAT TROUBLE WAS AFOOT.
NOW THAT YOU'VE ENJOYED SOME TEA, THE BANQUET IS READY. WON'T YOU COME WITH ME, PLEASE?
BIAN XI ... IT OCCURS TO ME THAT YOU MIGHT NOT HAVE THE BEST OF INTENTIONS.
WH ... WHAT?
HOW ***DARE*** YOU! SLAY ME WITH ***TRICKERY***? LIE TO MY FACE AND THEN ***AMBUSH*** ME LIKE A COWARDLY ***DOG***?
THE MEN WAITING OUTSIDE HEARD THE UNMISTAKABLE SOUNDS OF THEIR LEADER, BIAN XI, MEETING A VERY SUDDEN AND DECISIVE END.
IN HIS RAGE, GUAN YU STRUCK DOWN NOT ONLY BIAN XI BUT ALSO ALL OF HIS MEN.
GUAN YU THANKED PUJING FOR HELPING THEM, AND THEN HE TOOK LIU BEI'S WIVES AND LEFT.

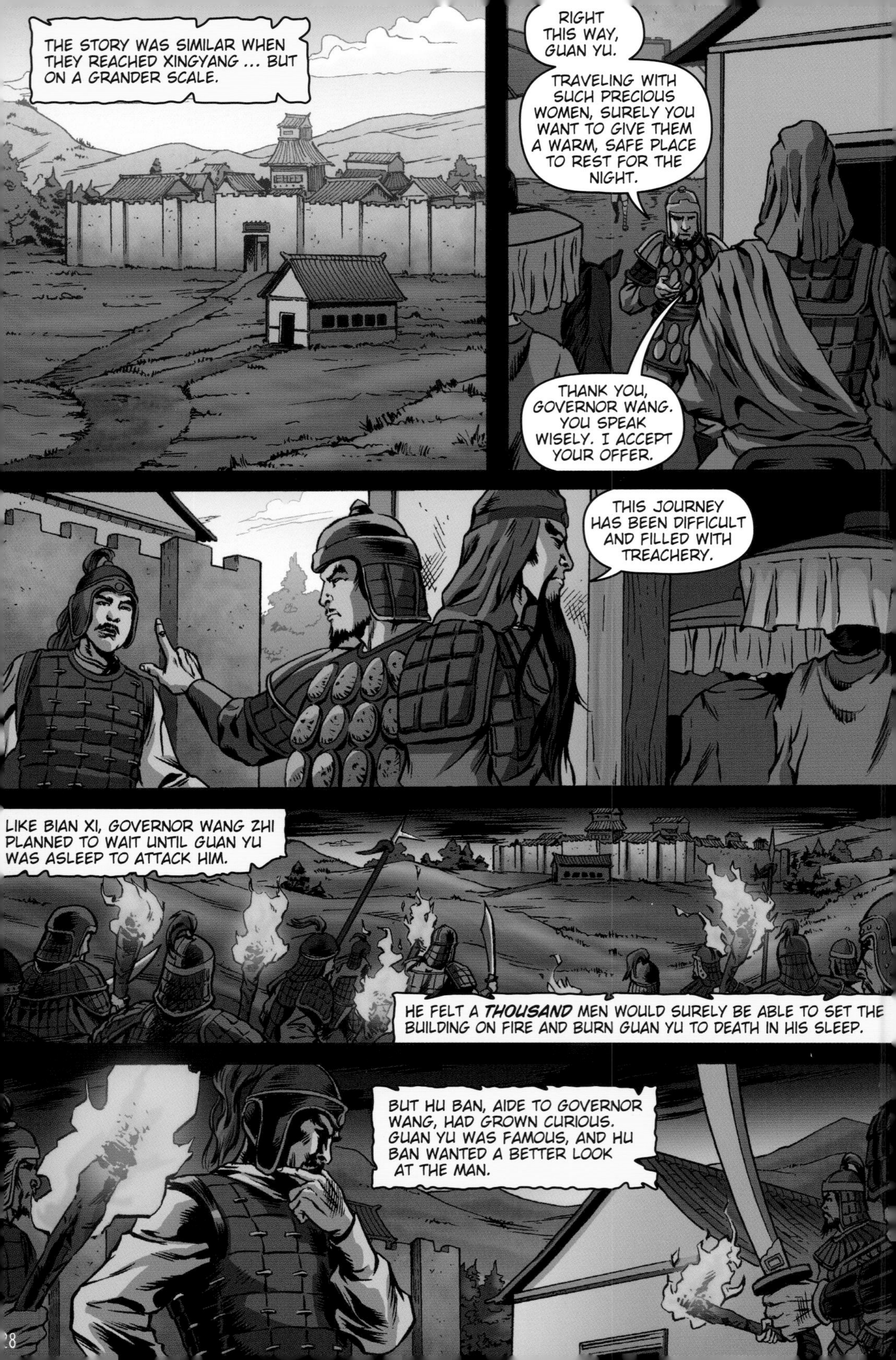
THE STORY WAS SIMILAR WHEN THEY REACHED XINGYANG ... BUT ON A GRANDER SCALE.
RIGHT THIS WAY, GUAN YU.
TRAVELING WITH SUCH PRECIOUS WOMEN, SURELY YOU WANT TO GIVE THEM A WARM, SAFE PLACE TO REST FOR THE NIGHT.
THANK YOU, GOVERNOR WANG. YOU SPEAK WISELY. I ACCEPT YOUR OFFER.
THIS JOURNEY HAS BEEN DIFFICULT AND FILLED WITH TREACHERY.
LIKE BIAN XI, GOVERNOR WANG ZHI PLANNED TO WAIT UNTIL GUAN YU WAS ASLEEP TO ATTACK HIM.
HE FELT A ***THOUSAND*** MEN WOULD SURELY BE ABLE TO SET THE BUILDING ON FIRE AND BURN GUAN YU TO DEATH IN HIS SLEEP.
BUT HU BAN, AIDE TO GOVERNOR WANG, HAD GROWN CURIOUS. GUAN YU WAS FAMOUS, AND HU BAN WANTED A BETTER LOOK AT THE MAN.

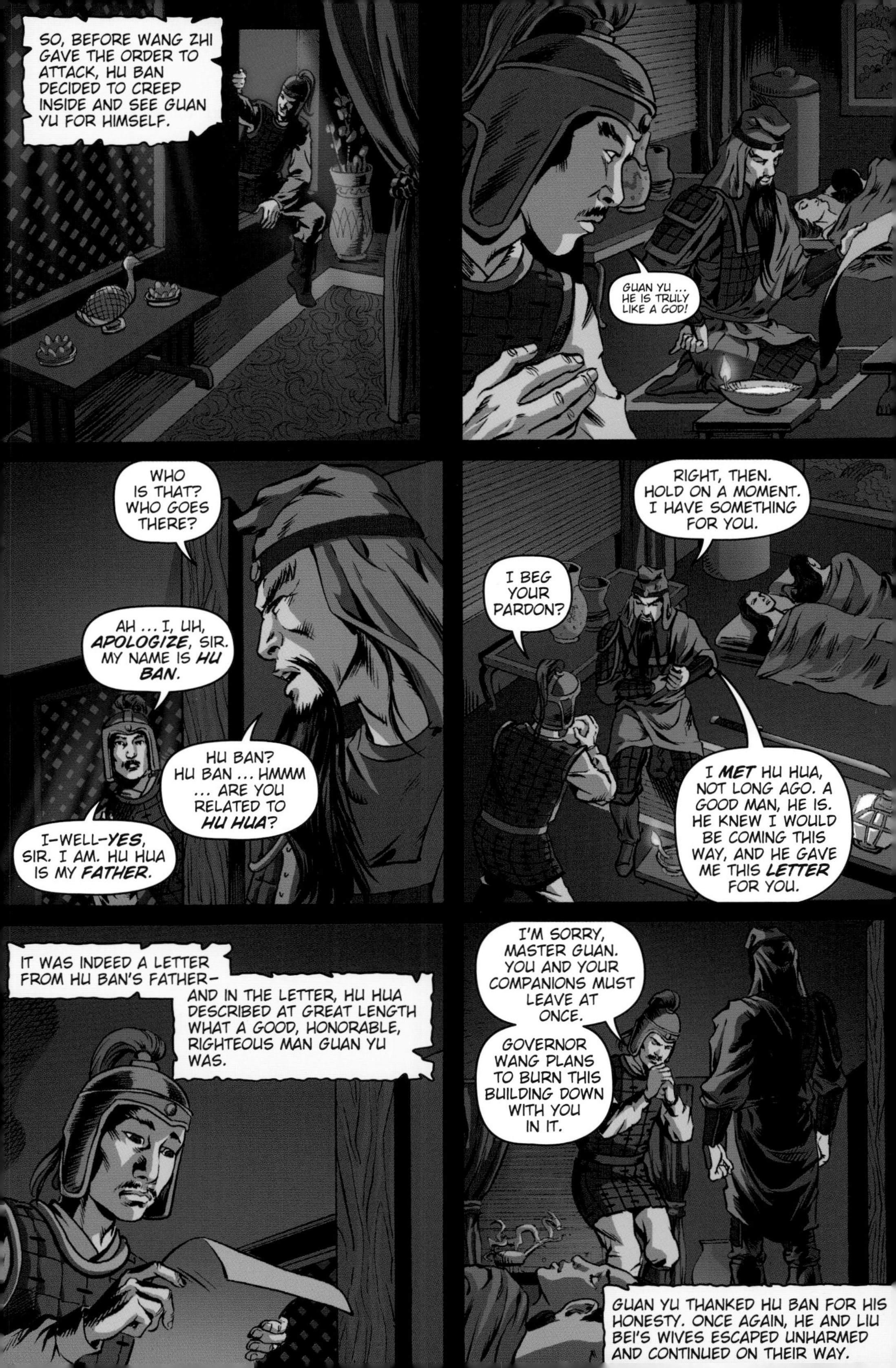
SO, BEFORE WANG ZHI GAVE THE ORDER TO ATTACK, HU BAN DECIDED TO CREEP INSIDE AND SEE GUAN YU FOR HIMSELF.
GUAN YU ... HE IS TRULY LIKE A GOD!
WHO IS THAT? WHO GOES THERE?
AH ... I, UH, APOLOGIZE, SIR. MY NAME IS HU BAN.
HU BAN? HU BAN ... HMMM ... ARE YOU RELATED TO HU HUA?
I-WELL-YES, SIR. I AM. HU HUA IS MY FATHER.
RIGHT, THEN. HOLD ON A MOMENT. I HAVE SOMETHING FOR YOU.
I BEG YOUR PARDON?
I MET HU HUA, NOT LONG AGO. A GOOD MAN, HE IS. HE KNEW I WOULD BE COMING THIS WAY, AND HE GAVE ME THIS LETTER FOR YOU.
IT WAS INDEED A LETTER FROM HU BAN'S FATHER—
AND IN THE LETTER, HU HUA DESCRIBED AT GREAT LENGTH WHAT A GOOD, HONORABLE, RIGHTEOUS MAN GUAN YU WAS.
I'M SORRY, MASTER GUAN. YOU AND YOUR COMPANIONS MUST LEAVE AT ONCE.
GOVERNOR WANG PLANS TO BURN THIS BUILDING DOWN WITH YOU IN IT.
GUAN YU THANKED HU BAN FOR HIS HONESTY. ONCE AGAIN, HE AND LIU BEI'S WIVES ESCAPED UNHARMED AND CONTINUED ON THEIR WAY.

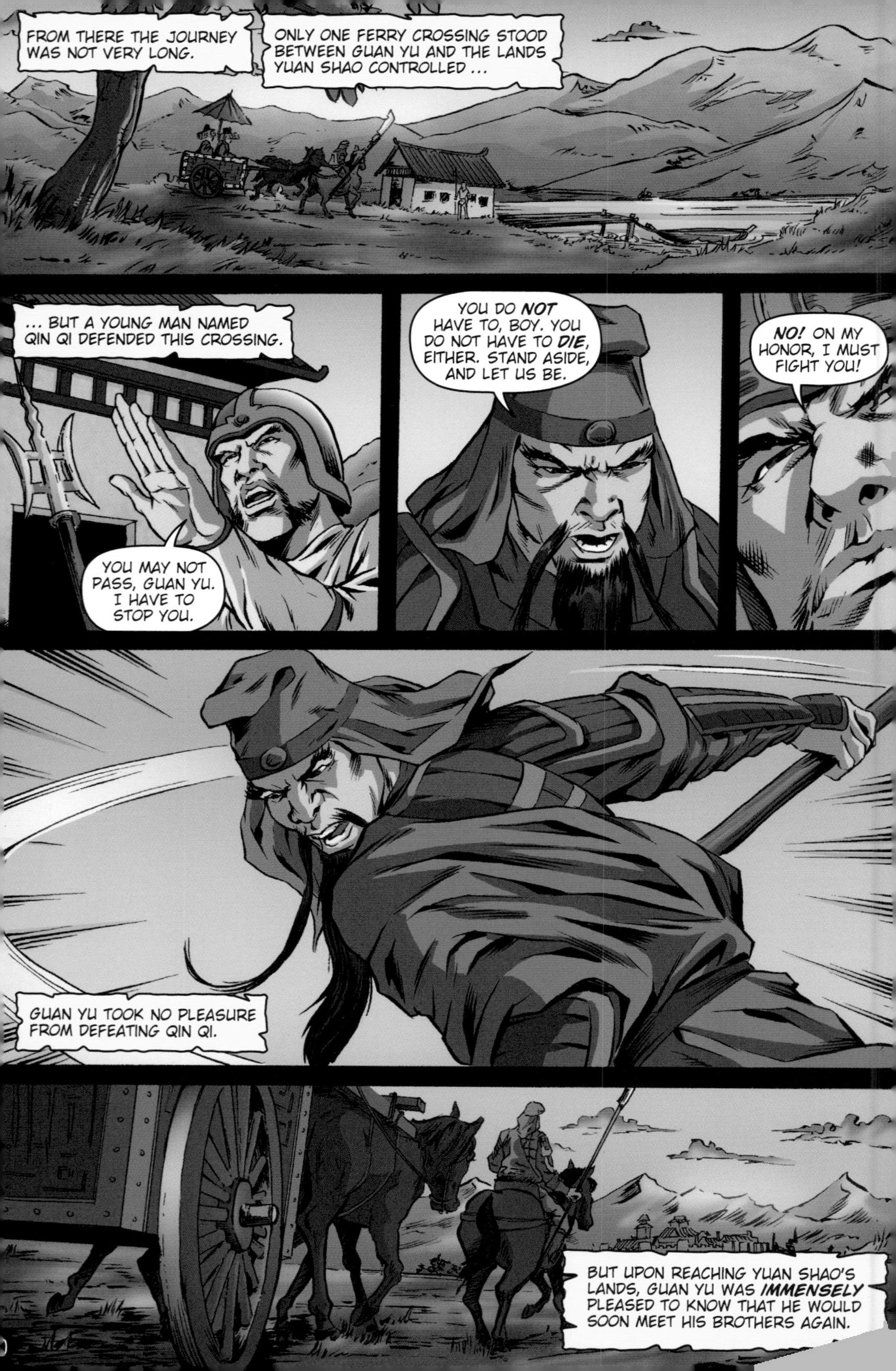
FROM THERE THE JOURNEY WAS NOT VERY LONG.
ONLY ONE FERRY CROSSING STOOD BETWEEN GUAN YU AND THE LANDS YUAN SHAO CONTROLLED ...
... BUT A YOUNG MAN NAMED QIN QI DEFENDED THIS CROSSING.
YOU MAY NOT PASS, GUAN YU. I HAVE TO STOP YOU.
YOU DO **NOT** HAVE TO, BOY. YOU DO NOT HAVE TO **DIE**, EITHER. STAND ASIDE, AND LET US BE.
NO! ON MY HONOR, I MUST FIGHT YOU!
GUAN YU TOOK NO PLEASURE FROM DEFEATING QIN QI.
BUT UPON REACHING YUAN SHAO'S LANDS, GUAN YU WAS **IMMENSELY** PLEASED TO KNOW THAT HE WOULD SOON MEET HIS BROTHERS AGAIN.

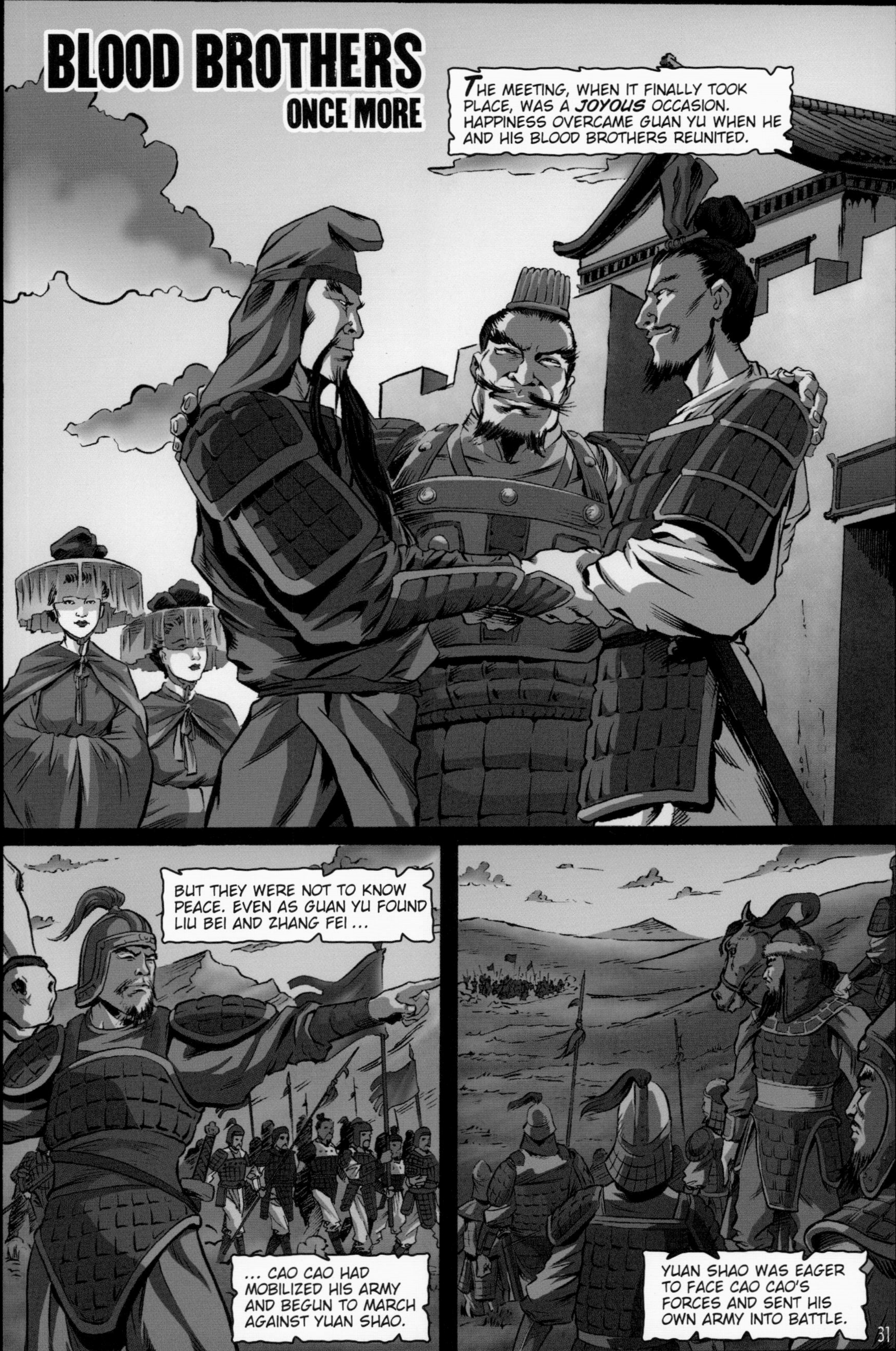
BLOOD BROTHERS ONCE MORE
THE MEETING, WHEN IT FINALLY TOOK PLACE, WAS A JOYOUS OCCASION. HAPPINESS OVERCAME GUAN YU WHEN HE AND HIS BLOOD BROTHERS REUNITED.
BUT THEY WERE NOT TO KNOW PEACE. EVEN AS GUAN YU FOUND LIU BEI AND ZHANG FEI ...
... CAO CAO HAD MOBILIZED HIS ARMY AND BEGUN TO MARCH AGAINST YUAN SHAO.
YUAN SHAO WAS EAGER TO FACE CAO CAO'S FORCES AND SENT HIS OWN ARMY INTO BATTLE.

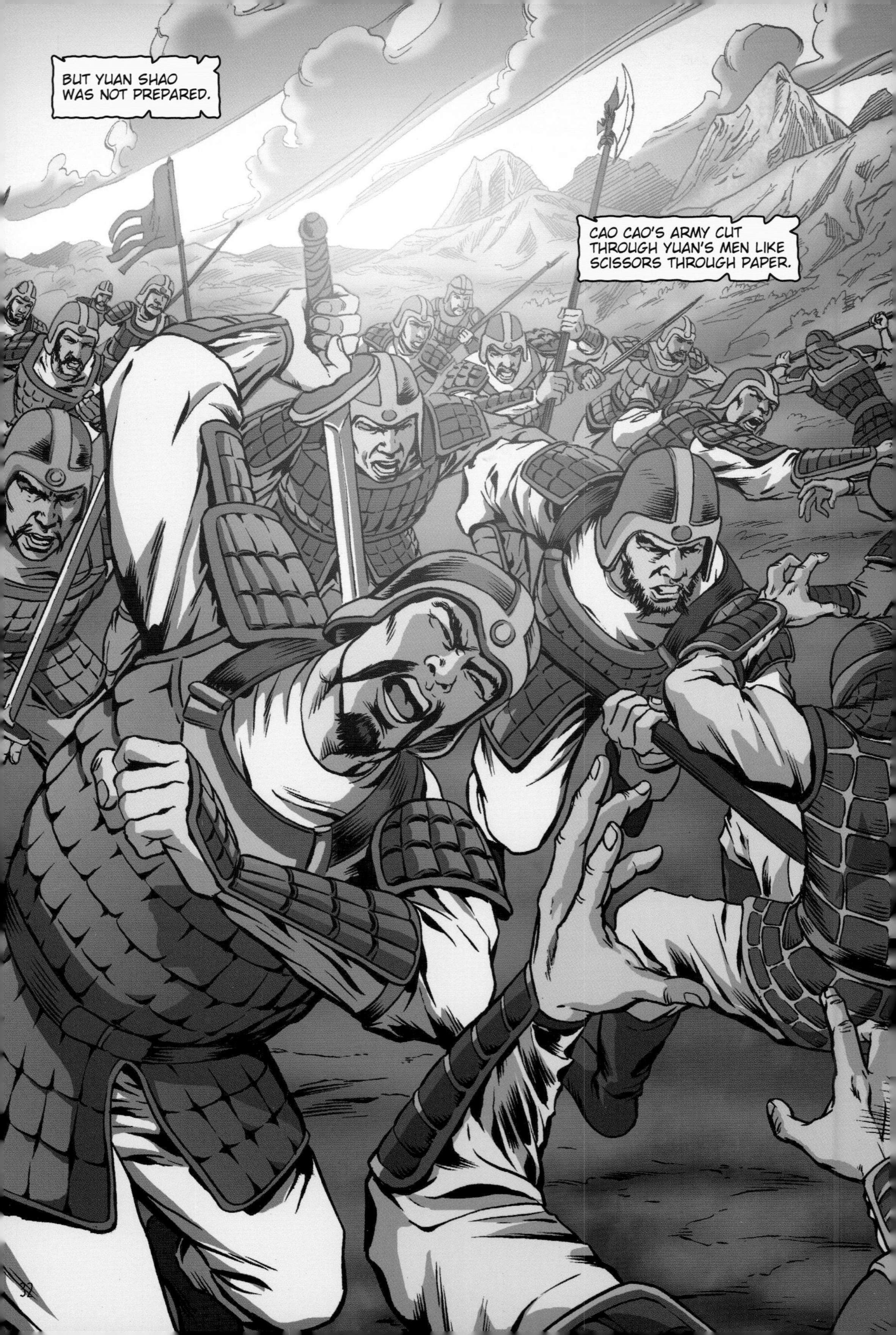
BUT YUAN SHAO WAS NOT PREPARED.
CAO CAO'S ARMY CUT THROUGH YUAN'S MEN LIKE SCISSORS THROUGH PAPER.

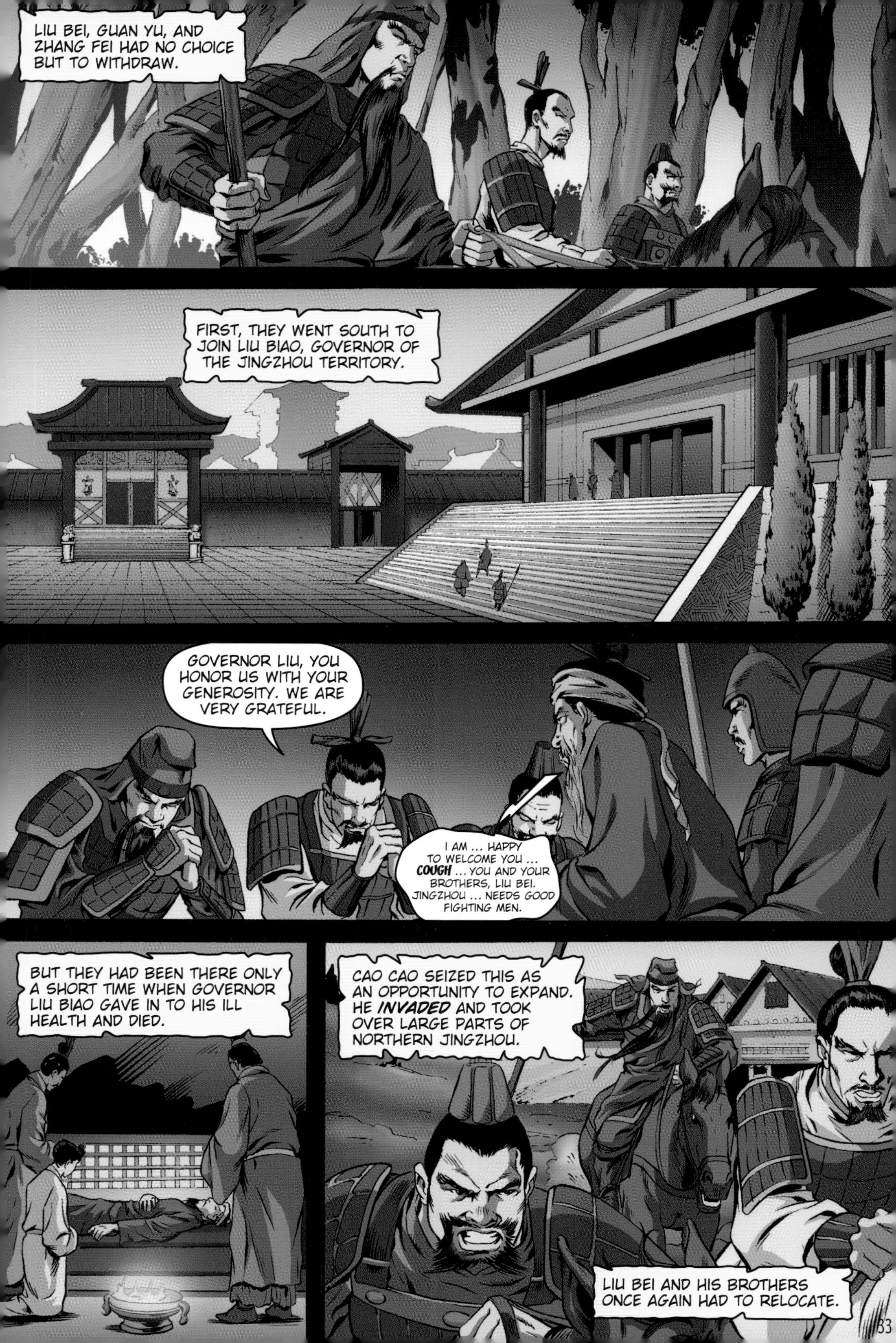
LIU BEI, GUAN YU, AND ZHANG FEI HAD NO CHOICE BUT TO WITHDRAW.
FIRST, THEY WENT SOUTH TO JOIN LIU BIAO, GOVERNOR OF THE JINGZHOU TERRITORY.
GOVERNOR LIU, YOU HONOR US WITH YOUR GENEROSITY. WE ARE VERY GRATEFUL.
I AM ... HAPPY TO WELCOME YOU ... COUGH ... YOU AND YOUR BROTHERS, LIU BEI. JINGZHOU ... NEEDS GOOD FIGHTING MEN.
BUT THEY HAD BEEN THERE ONLY A SHORT TIME WHEN GOVERNOR LIU BIAO GAVE IN TO HIS ILL HEALTH AND DIED.
CAO CAO SEIZED THIS AS AN OPPORTUNITY TO EXPAND. HE INVADED AND TOOK OVER LARGE PARTS OF NORTHERN JINGZHOU.
LIU BEI AND HIS BROTHERS ONCE AGAIN HAD TO RELOCATE.

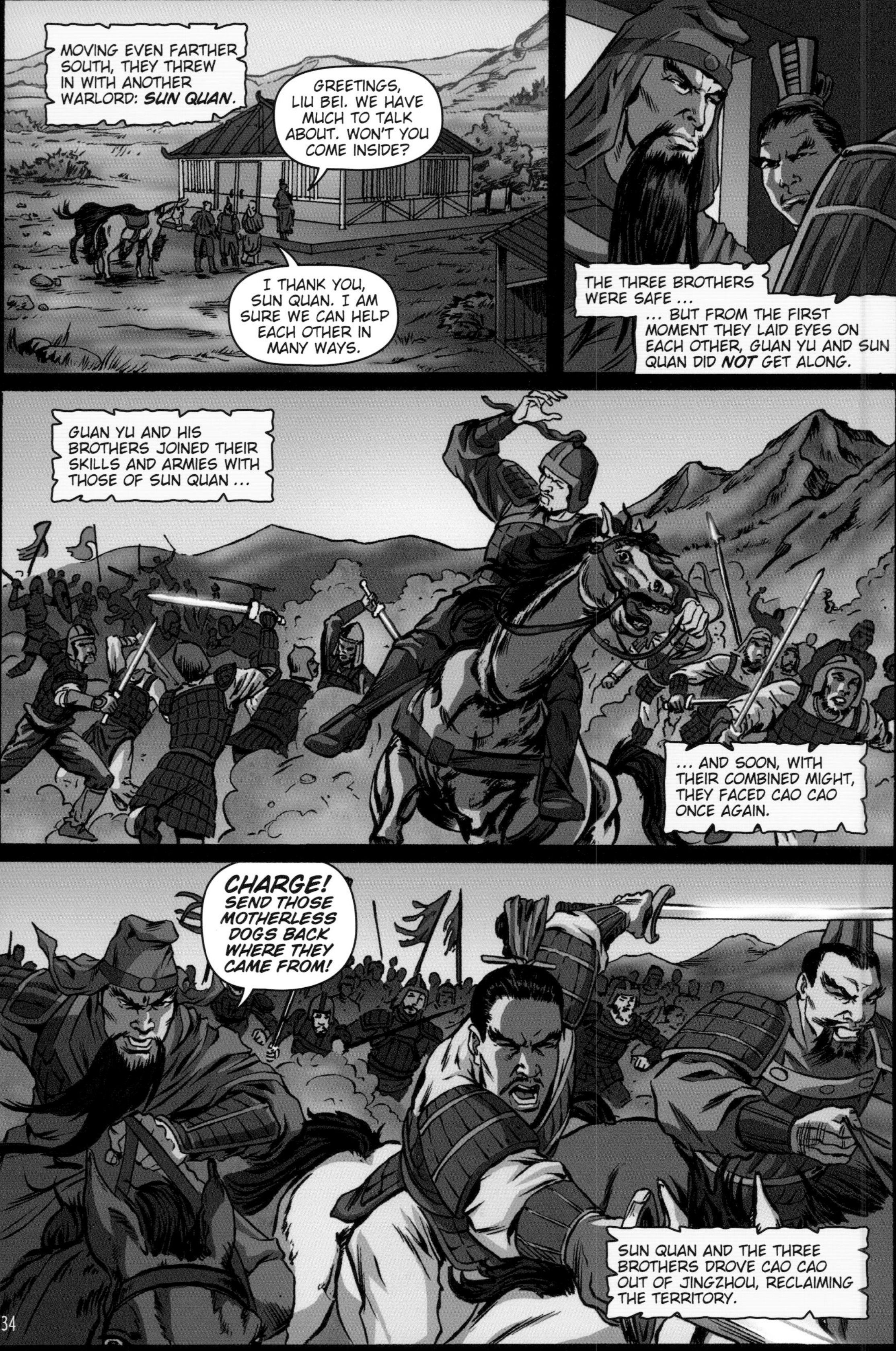
MOVING EVEN FARTHER SOUTH, THEY THREW IN WITH ANOTHER WARLORD: SUN QUAN.
GREETINGS, LIU BEI. WE HAVE MUCH TO TALK ABOUT. WON'T YOU COME INSIDE?
I THANK YOU, SUN QUAN. I AM SURE WE CAN HELP EACH OTHER IN MANY WAYS.
THE THREE BROTHERS WERE SAFE ...
... BUT FROM THE FIRST MOMENT THEY LAID EYES ON EACH OTHER, GUAN YU AND SUN QUAN DID NOT GET ALONG.
GUAN YU AND HIS BROTHERS JOINED THEIR SKILLS AND ARMIES WITH THOSE OF SUN QUAN ...
... AND SOON, WITH THEIR COMBINED MIGHT, THEY FACED CAO CAO ONCE AGAIN.
CHARGE! SEND THOSE MOTHERLESS DOGS BACK WHERE THEY CAME FROM!
SUN QUAN AND THE THREE BROTHERS DROVE CAO CAO OUT OF JINGZHOU, RECLAIMING THE TERRITORY.

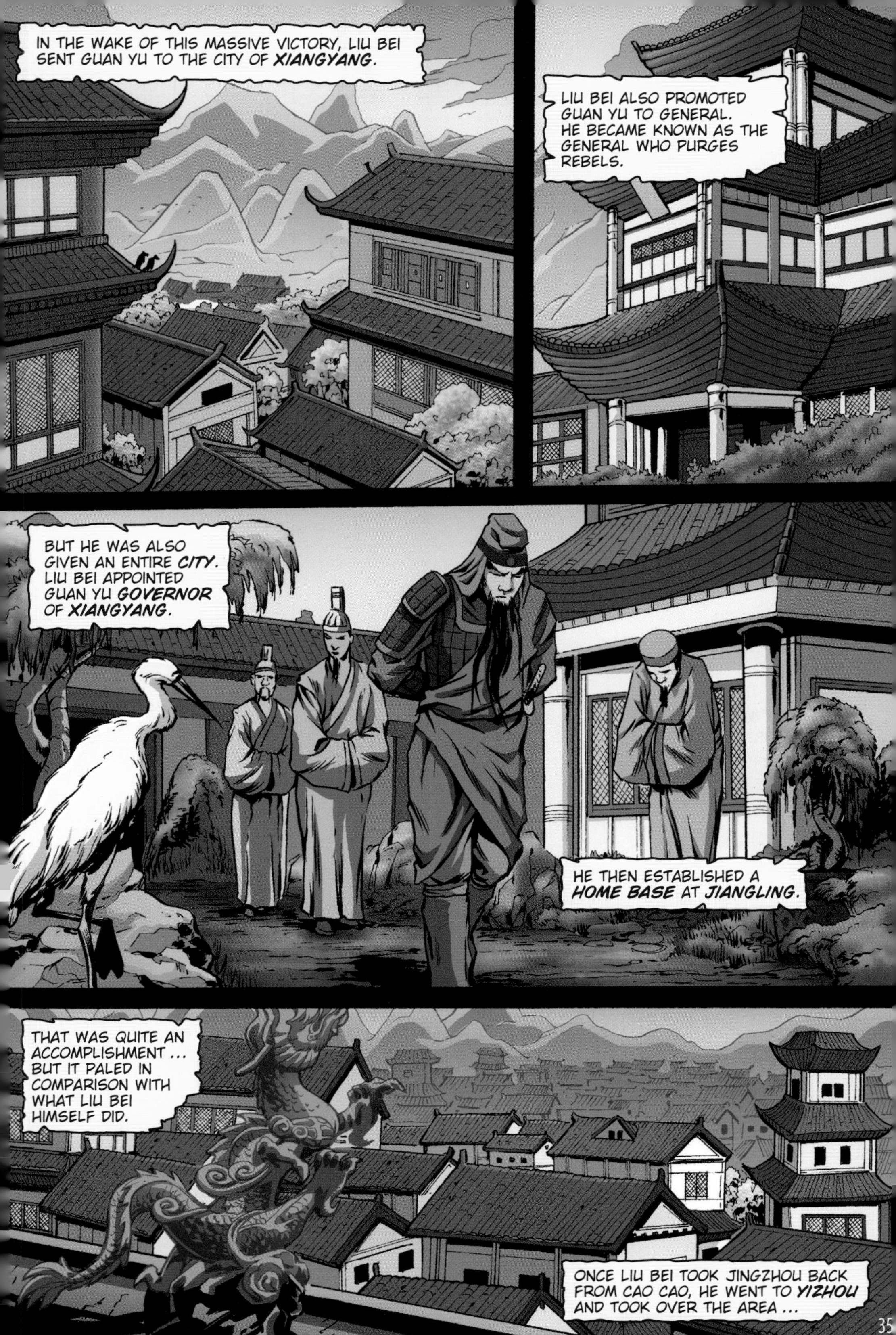
IN THE WAKE OF THIS MASSIVE VICTORY, LIU BEI SENT GUAN YU TO THE CITY OF XIANGYANG.
LIU BEI ALSO PROMOTED GUAN YU TO GENERAL. HE BECAME KNOWN AS THE GENERAL WHO PURGES REBELS.
BUT HE WAS ALSO GIVEN AN ENTIRE CITY. LIU BEI APPOINTED GUAN YU GOVERNOR OF XIANGYANG.
HE THEN ESTABLISHED A HOME BASE AT JIANGLING.
THAT WAS QUITE AN ACCOMPLISHMENT ... BUT IT PALED IN COMPARISON WITH WHAT LIU BEI HIMSELF DID.
ONCE LIU BEI TOOK JINGZHOU BACK FROM CAO CAO, HE WENT TO YIZHOU AND TOOK OVER THE AREA ...

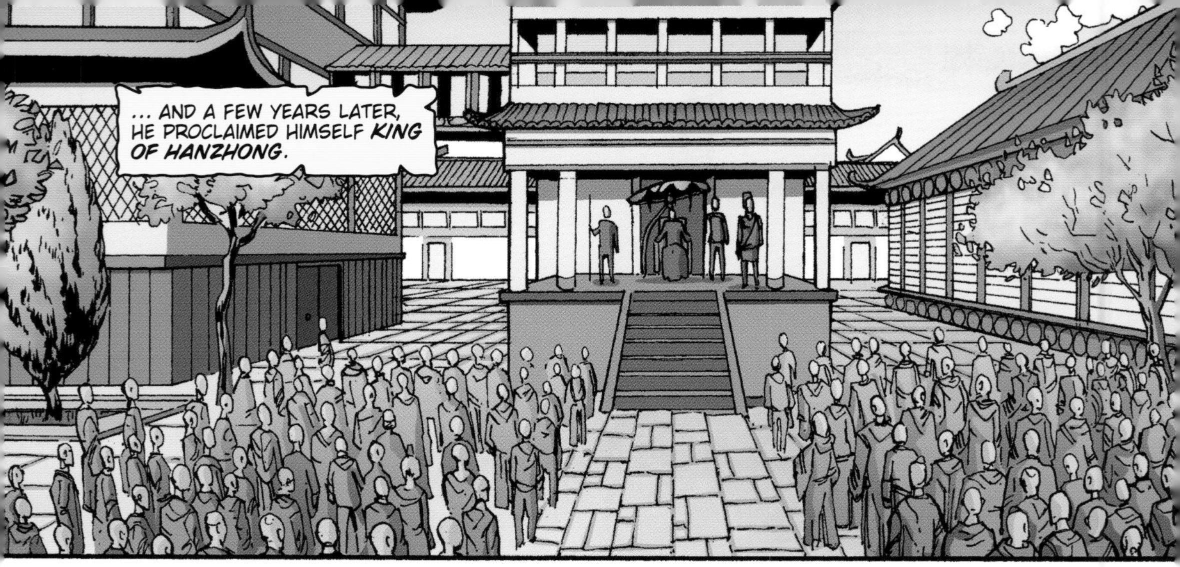
... AND A FEW YEARS LATER, HE PROCLAIMED HIMSELF KING OF HANZHONG.

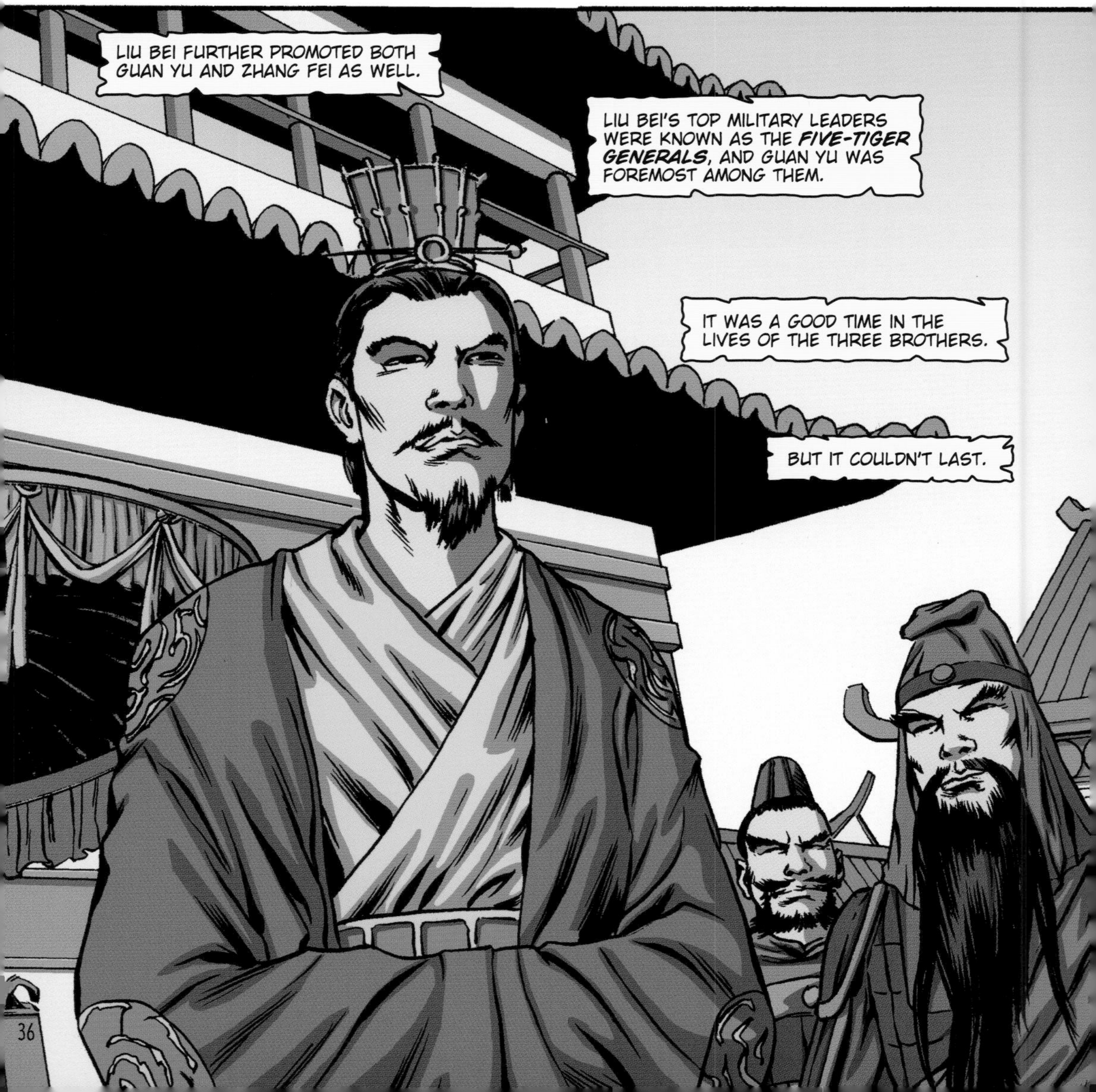
LIU BEI FURTHER PROMOTED BOTH GUAN YU AND ZHANG FEI AS WELL.
LIU BEI'S TOP MILITARY LEADERS WERE KNOWN AS THE FIVE-TIGER GENERALS, AND GUAN YU WAS FOREMOST AMONG THEM.
IT WAS A GOOD TIME IN THE LIVES OF THE THREE BROTHERS.
BUT IT COULDN'T LAST.

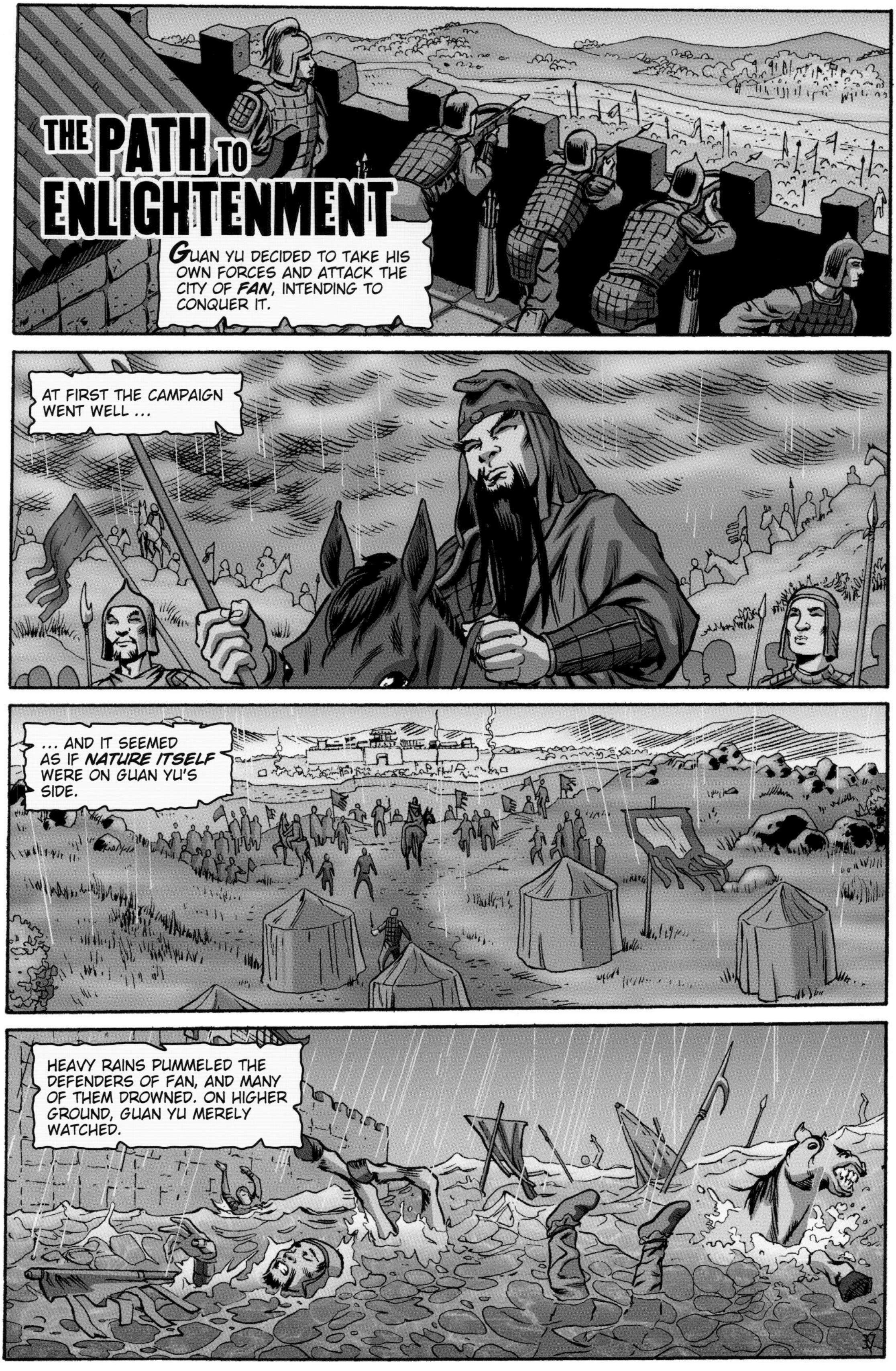
THE PATH TO ENLIGHTENMENT
GUAN YU DECIDED TO TAKE HIS OWN FORCES AND ATTACK THE CITY OF FAN, INTENDING TO CONQUER IT.
AT FIRST THE CAMPAIGN WENT WELL ...
... AND IT SEEMED AS IF NATURE ITSELF WERE ON GUAN YU'S SIDE.
HEAVY RAINS PUMMELED THE DEFENDERS OF FAN, AND MANY OF THEM DROWNED. ON HIGHER GROUND, GUAN YU MERELY WATCHED.

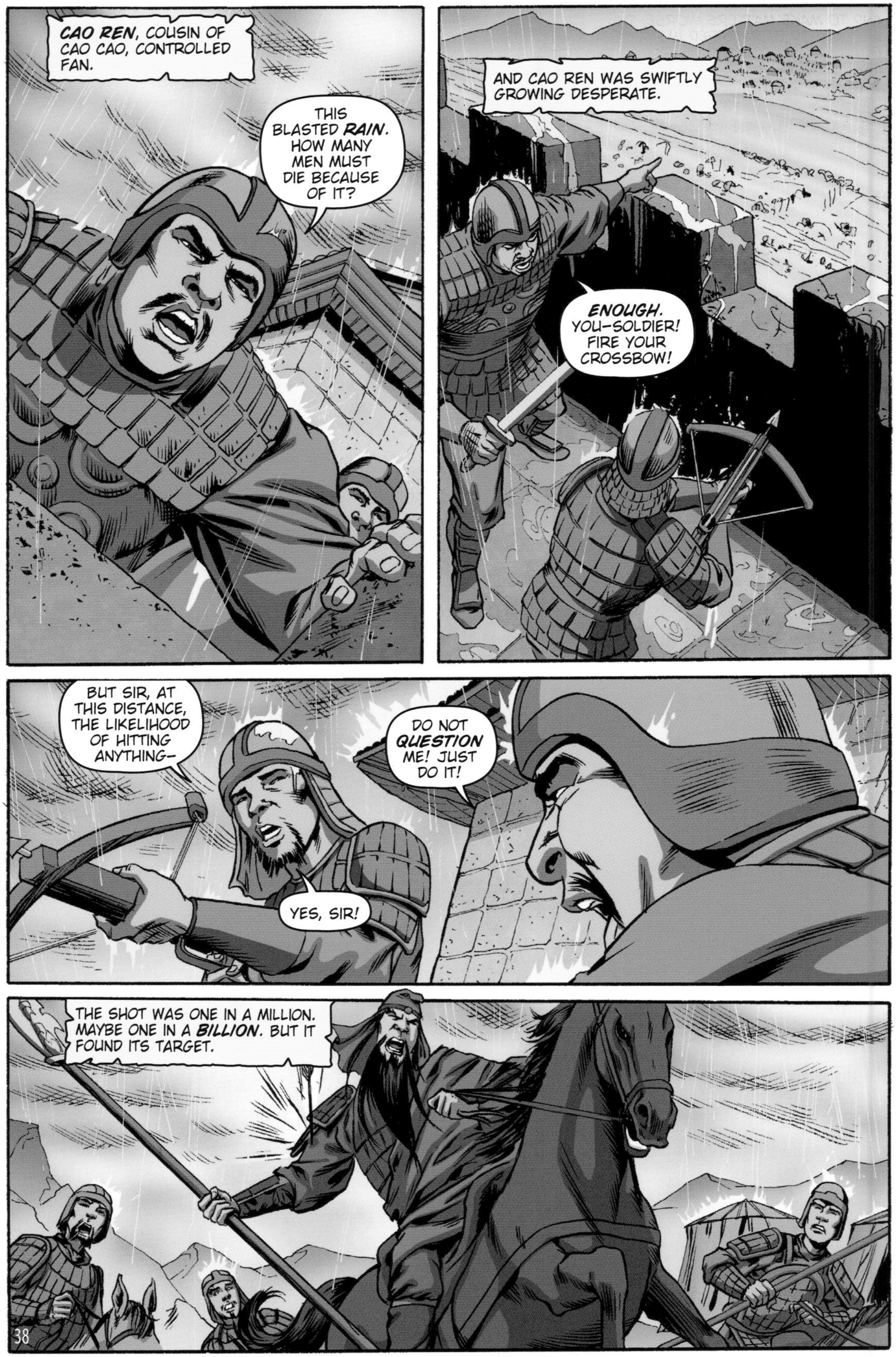
CAO REN, COUSIN OF CAO CAO, CONTROLLED FAN.
THIS BLASTED RAIN. HOW MANY MEN MUST DIE BECAUSE OF IT?
AND CAO REN WAS SWIFTLY GROWING DESPERATE.
ENOUGH. YOU–SOLDIER! FIRE YOUR CROSSBOW!
BUT SIR, AT THIS DISTANCE, THE LIKELIHOOD OF HITTING ANYTHING–
DO NOT QUESTION ME! JUST DO IT!
YES, SIR!
THE SHOT WAS ONE IN A MILLION. MAYBE ONE IN A BILLION. BUT IT FOUND ITS TARGET.

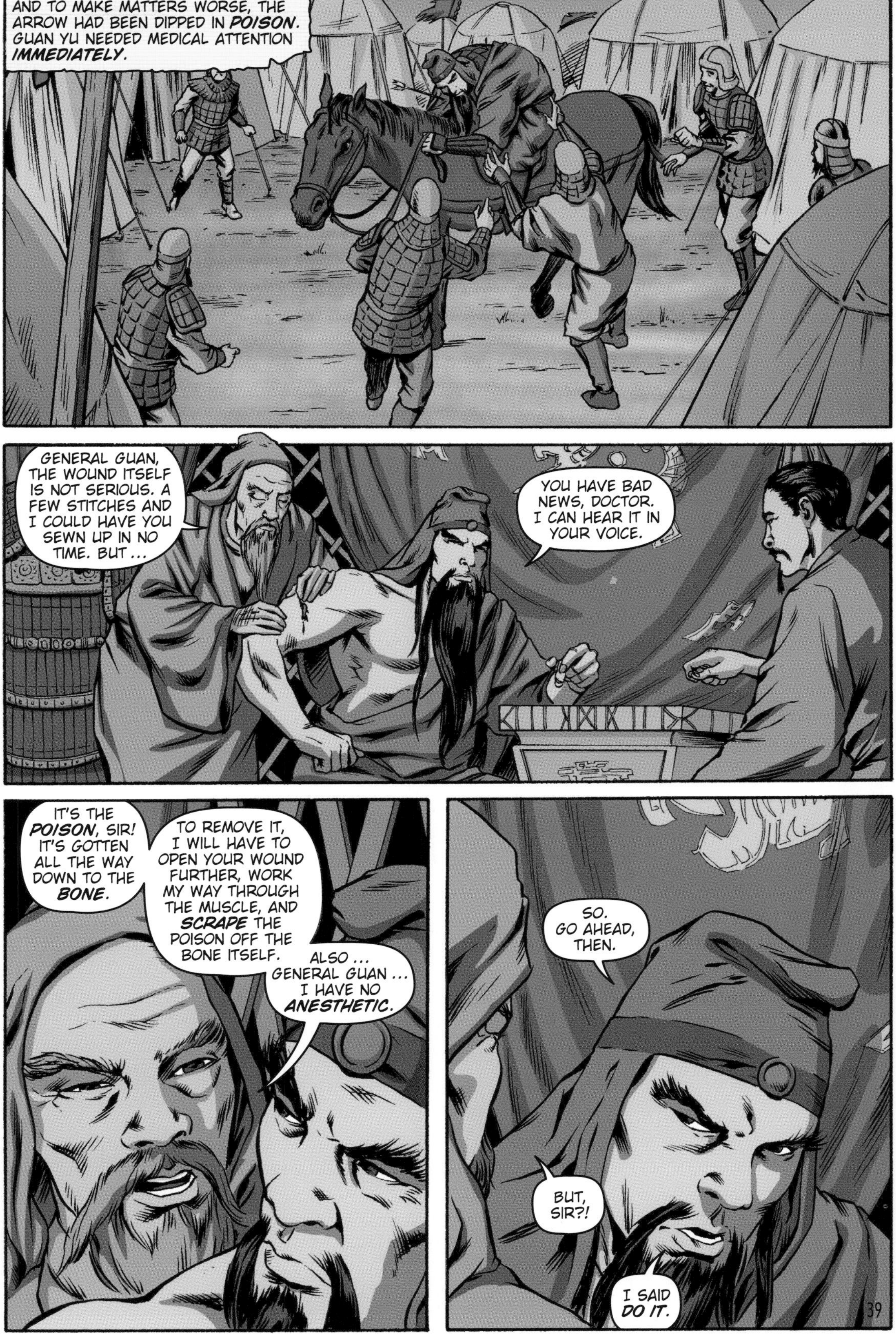

AND TO MAKE MATTERS WORSE, THE ARROW HAD BEEN DIPPED IN *POISON*. GUAN YU NEEDED MEDICAL ATTENTION *IMMEDIATELY*.
GENERAL GUAN, THE WOUND ITSELF IS NOT SERIOUS. A FEW STITCHES AND I COULD HAVE YOU SEWN UP IN NO TIME. BUT ...
YOU HAVE BAD NEWS, DOCTOR. I CAN HEAR IT IN YOUR VOICE.
IT'S THE *POISON*, SIR! IT'S GOTTEN ALL THE WAY DOWN TO THE *BONE*.
TO REMOVE IT, I WILL HAVE TO OPEN YOUR WOUND FURTHER, WORK MY WAY THROUGH THE MUSCLE, AND *SCRAPE* THE POISON OFF THE BONE ITSELF.
ALSO ... GENERAL GUAN ... I HAVE NO *ANESTHETIC*.
SO. GO AHEAD, THEN.
BUT, SIR?!
I SAID *DO IT*.

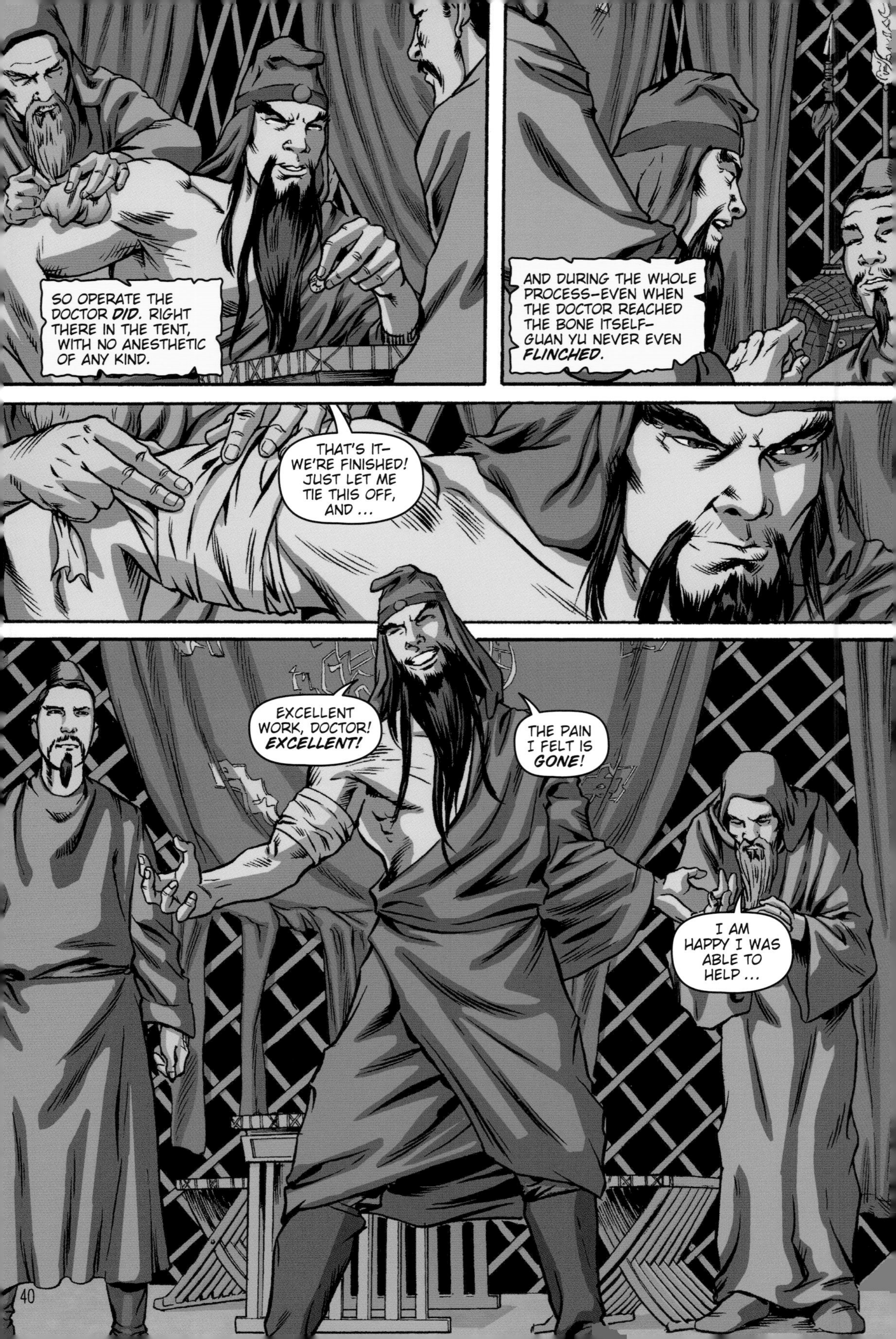
SO OPERATE THE DOCTOR ***DID***. RIGHT THERE IN THE TENT, WITH NO ANESTHETIC OF ANY KIND.
AND DURING THE WHOLE PROCESS—EVEN WHEN THE DOCTOR REACHED THE BONE ITSELF—GUAN YU NEVER EVEN ***FLINCHED***.
THAT'S IT—WE'RE FINISHED! JUST LET ME TIE THIS OFF, AND …
EXCELLENT WORK, DOCTOR! ***EXCELLENT!***
THE PAIN I FELT IS ***GONE***!
I AM HAPPY I WAS ABLE TO HELP …

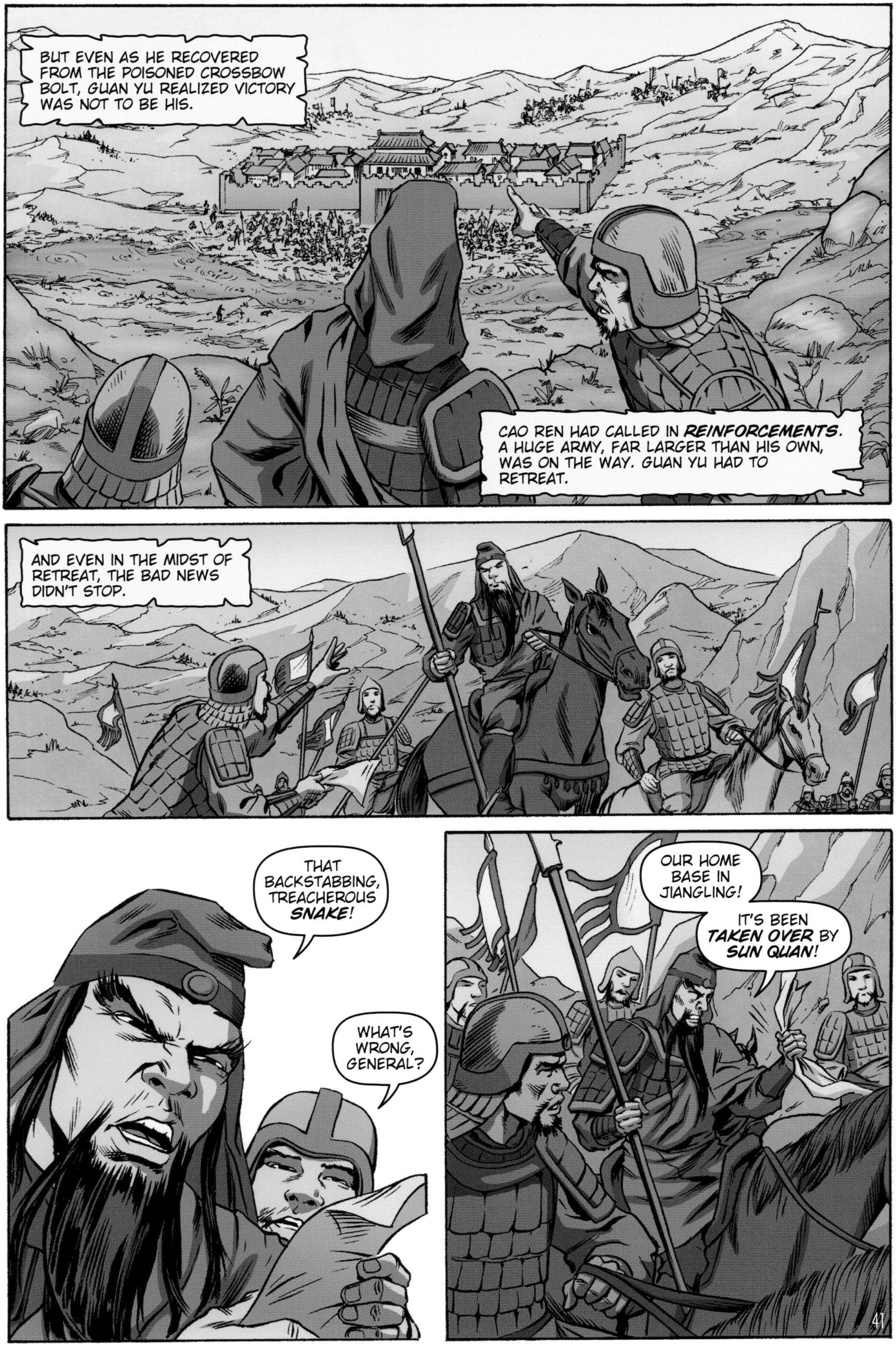
BUT EVEN AS HE RECOVERED FROM THE POISONED CROSSBOW BOLT, GUAN YU REALIZED VICTORY WAS NOT TO BE HIS.
CAO REN HAD CALLED IN REINFORCEMENTS. A HUGE ARMY, FAR LARGER THAN HIS OWN, WAS ON THE WAY. GUAN YU HAD TO RETREAT.
AND EVEN IN THE MIDST OF RETREAT, THE BAD NEWS DIDN'T STOP.
THAT BACKSTABBING, TREACHEROUS SNAKE!
WHAT'S WRONG, GENERAL?
OUR HOME BASE IN JIANGLING!
IT'S BEEN TAKEN OVER BY SUN QUAN!

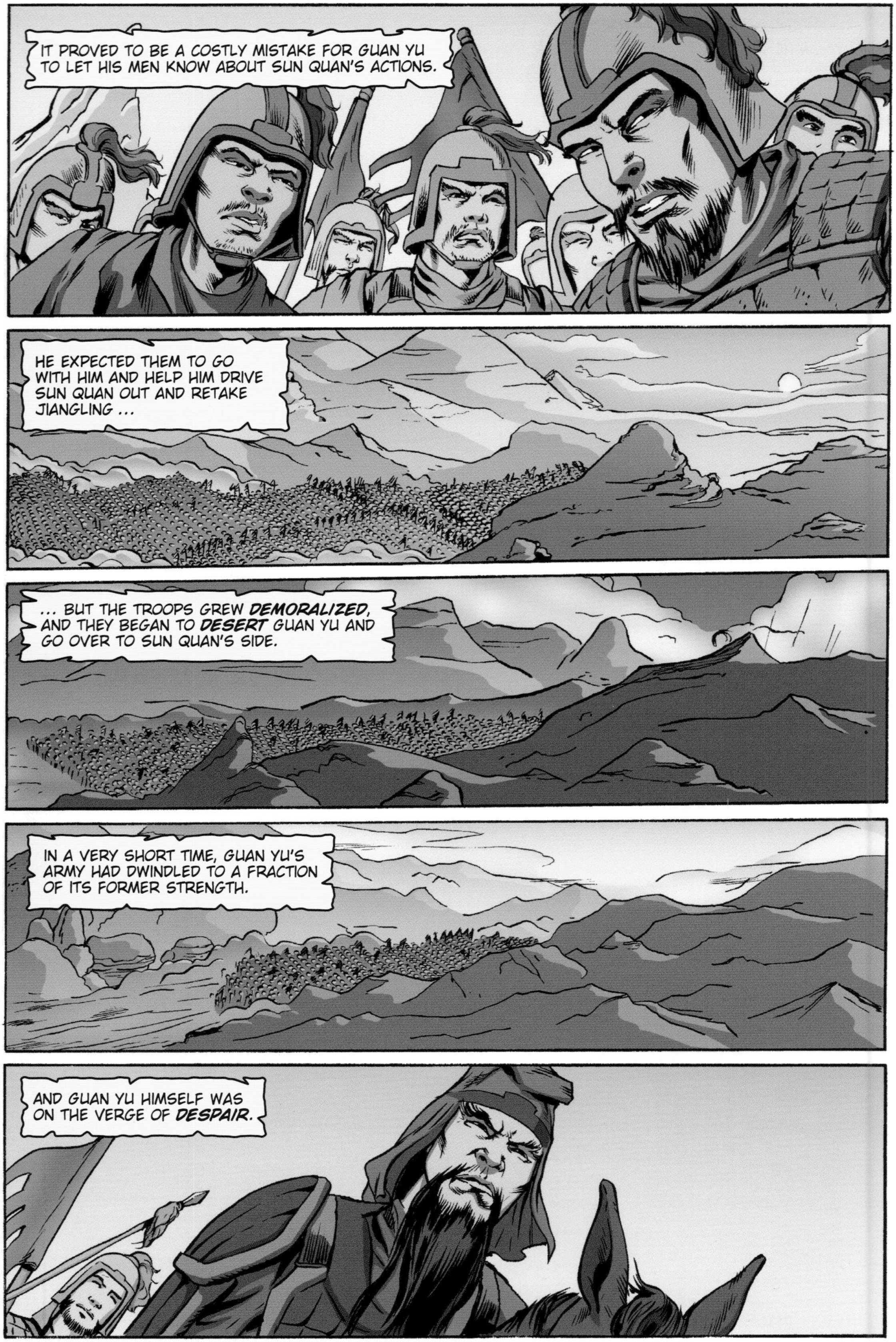
IT PROVED TO BE A COSTLY MISTAKE FOR GUAN YU TO LET HIS MEN KNOW ABOUT SUN QUAN'S ACTIONS.
HE EXPECTED THEM TO GO WITH HIM AND HELP HIM DRIVE SUN QUAN OUT AND RETAKE JIANGLING ...
... BUT THE TROOPS GREW DEMORALIZED, AND THEY BEGAN TO DESERT GUAN YU AND GO OVER TO SUN QUAN'S SIDE.
IN A VERY SHORT TIME, GUAN YU'S ARMY HAD DWINDLED TO A FRACTION OF ITS FORMER STRENGTH.
AND GUAN YU HIMSELF WAS ON THE VERGE OF DESPAIR.

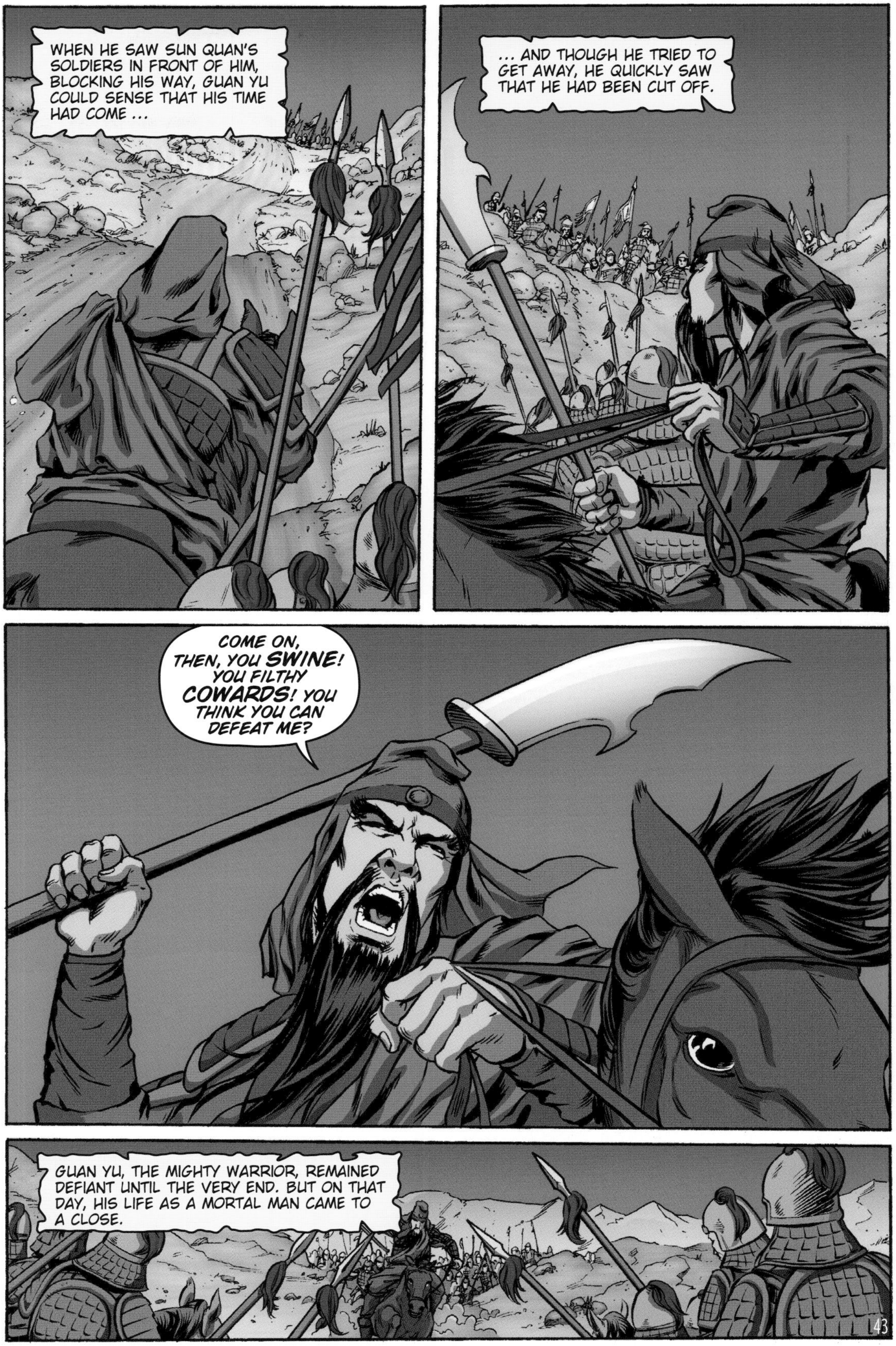
WHEN HE SAW SUN QUAN'S SOLDIERS IN FRONT OF HIM, BLOCKING HIS WAY, GUAN YU COULD SENSE THAT HIS TIME HAD COME ...
... AND THOUGH HE TRIED TO GET AWAY, HE QUICKLY SAW THAT HE HAD BEEN CUT OFF.
COME ON, THEN, YOU SWINE! YOU FILTHY COWARDS! YOU THINK YOU CAN DEFEAT ME?
GUAN YU, THE MIGHTY WARRIOR, REMAINED DEFIANT UNTIL THE VERY END. BUT ON THAT DAY, HIS LIFE AS A MORTAL MAN CAME TO A CLOSE.

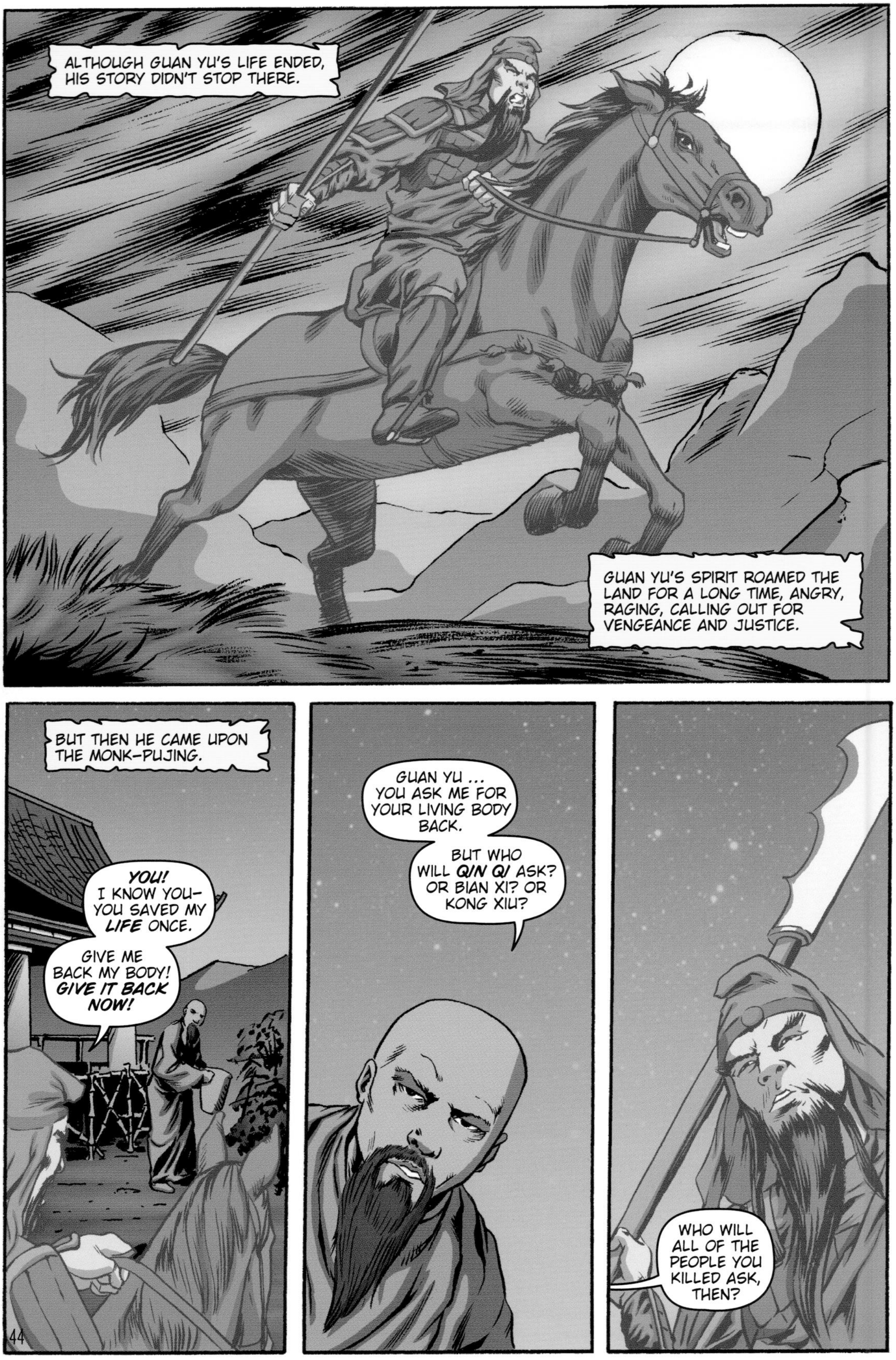
ALTHOUGH GUAN YU'S LIFE ENDED, HIS STORY DIDN'T STOP THERE.
GUAN YU'S SPIRIT ROAMED THE LAND FOR A LONG TIME, ANGRY, RAGING, CALLING OUT FOR VENGEANCE AND JUSTICE.
BUT THEN HE CAME UPON THE MONK-PUJING.
YOU! I KNOW YOU- YOU SAVED MY LIFE ONCE.
GIVE ME BACK MY BODY! GIVE IT BACK NOW!
GUAN YU ... YOU ASK ME FOR YOUR LIVING BODY BACK.
BUT WHO WILL QIN QI ASK? OR BIAN XI? OR KONG XIU?
WHO WILL ALL OF THE PEOPLE YOU KILLED ASK, THEN?

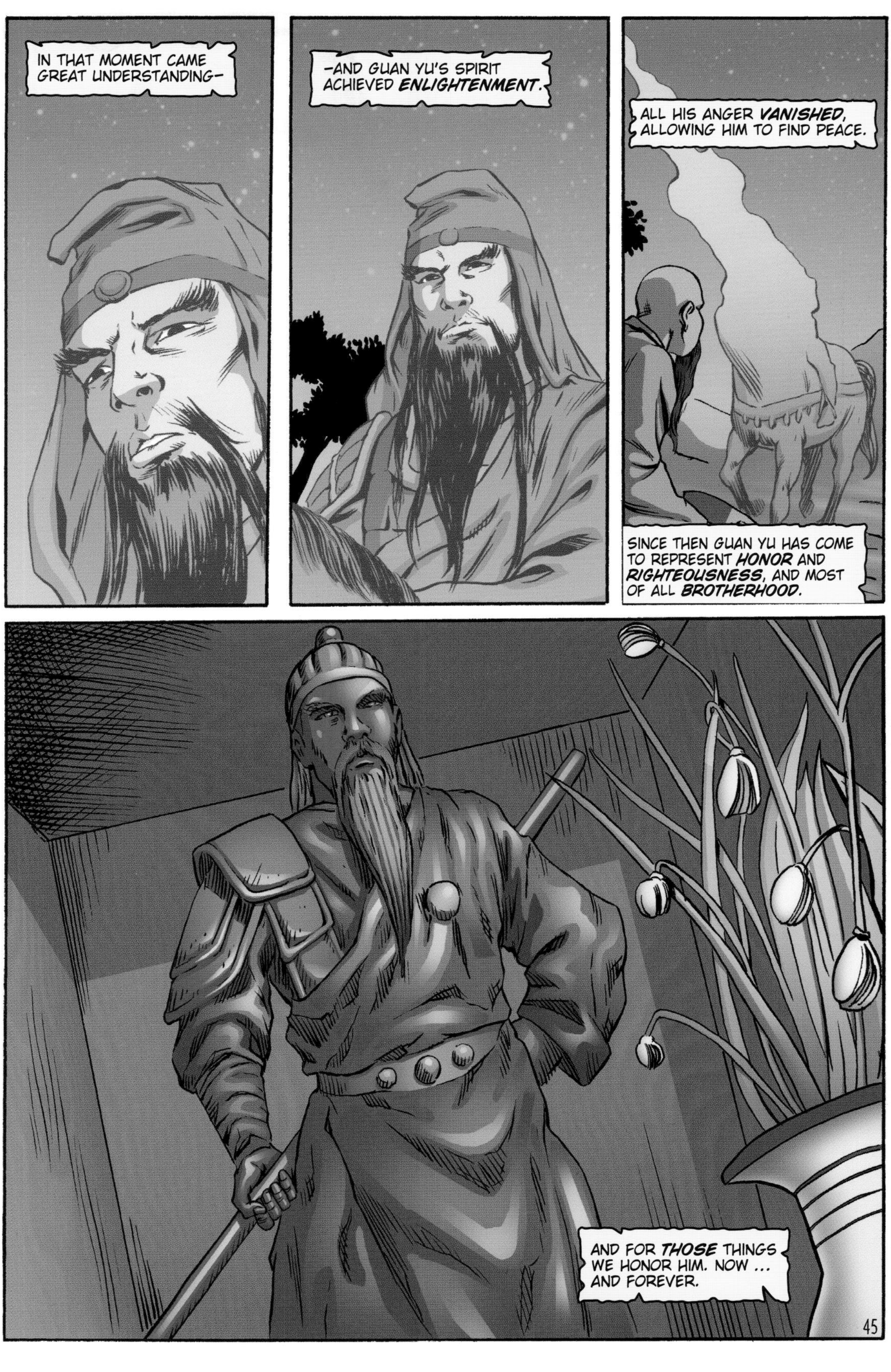
IN THAT MOMENT CAME GREAT UNDERSTANDING–
–AND GUAN YU'S SPIRIT ACHIEVED ENLIGHTENMENT.
ALL HIS ANGER VANISHED, ALLOWING HIM TO FIND PEACE.
SINCE THEN GUAN YU HAS COME TO REPRESENT HONOR AND RIGHTEOUSNESS, AND MOST OF ALL BROTHERHOOD.
AND FOR THOSE THINGS WE HONOR HIM. NOW ... AND FOREVER.

GLOSSARY AND PRONUNCIATION GUIDE

AMBUSH: to hide and attack someone by surprise

BLOOD BROTHERS: men who have pledged their loyalty to one another

ENLIGHTENMENT: a peaceful condition in which one feels no suffering or desire

GUAN DAO: a weapon that consists of a curved blade on a long pole

GUAN YU (*gwan yoo*): an ancient Chinese warrior. Guan Yu is an important figure in *The Romance of the Three Kingdoms*, a historical novel that tells exaggerated stories about his life.

LIU BEI (*lee-o bay*): a soldier under whom Guan Yu served. In *The Romance of the Three Kingdoms*, Liu Bei was one of Guan Yu's blood brothers.

MONK: a man who has devoted his life to his religion

MORTAL: a human being, or a being that dies

SIEGE: an attack. To lay siege to a place is to surround it with armed forces.

VENGEANCE (*ven*-juhns): action taken to pay someone back for causing harm

YELLOW SCARVES: a group of peasants that rebelled against the Chinese government in A.D. 184. This group was named for the yellow scarves its members wore.

ZHANG FEI (*jahng fay*): a warrior who served under Liu Bei. In *The Romance of the Three Kingdoms*, Zhang Fei was one of Guan Yu's blood brothers.

original pencil sketch from page 20

FURTHER READING AND WEBSITES

Hume, Lotta Carswell. *Favorite Children's Stories from China and Tibet*. Boston: Tuttle Publishing, 2004. In this illustrated collection, you'll find traditional tales such as *A Chinese Cinderella*, *The Wishing Cup*, and *The Little Hare's Clever Trick*.

Simonds, Nina, Leslie Swartz, and the Children's Museum, Boston. *Moonbeams, Dumplings and Dragon Boats: A Treasury of Chinese Holiday Tales, Activities and Recipes*. San Diego: Harcourt, 2002. Learn about Chinese traditions and holidays through stories, recipes, games, and crafts.

Williams, Suzanne. *Made in China: Ideas and Inventions from Ancient China*. Berkeley, CA: Pacific View Press, 1996. The compass, the abacus, paper, and silk—all these things were invented in China. Learn about these and other Chinese inventions in this fascinating book.

The British Museum: Ancient China
http://www.ancientchina.co.uk/menu.html
This website from the British Museum includes information on five different topics important in ancient Chinese history. It also features several stories and narratives relevant to each of the topics.

China: An Inner Realm
http://library.thinkquest.org/20443/g_home.html
This site is a rich resource for exploring the land, culture, and language of China.

CREATING *GUAN YU: BLOOD BROTHERS TO THE END*

The story of Guan Yu was adapted primarily from *Three Kingdoms: A Historical Novel*, translated by Moss Roberts. Author Dan Jolley wrote the tale in consultation with Wang Ping, PhD, Associate Professor of English at Macalester College, and Wen-Hua Du, MA, of the Department of Foreign Languages and Linguistics at the University of Wisconsin-Milwaukee. Artist Ron Randall relied on numerous historical resources and worked collaboratively with Wang Ping in shaping the story's visual content.

INDEX

ABOUT THE AUTHOR AND THE ARTIST

DAN JOLLEY began his writing career in the early nineties. His limited series *Obergeist* was voted Best Horror Comic of 2001 by *Wizard Magazine*, and his DC Comics project *JSA: The Unholy Three* received an Eisner Award nomination (the comics industry's highest honor) for Best Limited Series of 2003. In recent years, he has cowritten two novels based on licensed properties: *Star Trek SCE: Some Assembly Required*, and *Vengeance*, from the television series *Angel*. May of 2007 saw the debut of Jolley's first solo novel series, an original young adult sci-fi espionage story called *Alex, Unlimited*, published by a joint venture of TokyoPop and HarperCollins. Jolley lives in Cary, North Carolina, where he spends way too much time playing video games.

RON RANDALL has drawn comics for every major comic publisher in the United States, including Marvel, DC, Image, and Dark Horse. His myths and legends work includes *Thor and Loki: In the Land of the Giants*. He has also worked on superhero comics such as *Justice League* and *Spiderman*; science fiction titles such as *Star Wars* and *Star Trek*; fantasy adventure titles such as *DragonLance* and *Warlord*; suspense and horror titles including *SwampThing*, *Predator*, and *Venom*; and his own creation, *Trekker*. He lives in Portland, Oregon.